SRA
Teacher's Resource Book

McGraw Hill **SRA**

Columbus, OH

SRAonline.com

 SRA

Send all inquiries to this address:
SRA/McGraw-Hill
4400 Easton Commons
Columbus, OH 43219

ISBN: 978-0-07-611230-2
MHID: 0-07-611230-6

2 3 4 5 6 7 8 9 BCM 13 12 11 10 09 08

The **McGraw-Hill** Companies

Contents

SRA Corrective Reading

Develop Struggling Readers' Skills, Grades 3–Adult

For struggling students, the consistently explicit, sequential, and systematic instruction using *Corrective Reading* promises:

- Accurate, efficient, effective learning
- Skill mastery for every student
- Heightened academic achievement

Corrective Reading Meets the Needs of At-Risk Students

Today, fully one-third of students—those reading below the 35th percentile on national, norm-referenced tests—cannot read at a level required to understand grade-level textbooks.

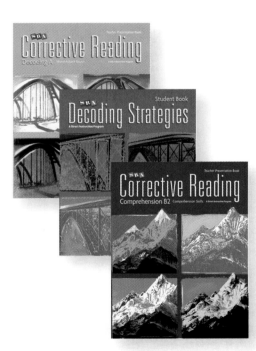

**Corrective Reading
Decoding and Comprehension**

Analyses by the Education Trust* show disturbing achievement discrepancies between students of color and low-income students compared to white and more affluent students.

- Only 13% of African American fourth graders reach proficient or advanced levels on the National Assessment of Educational Progress (NAEP), while 59% have not achieved the basic level.
- Only 15% of Latino fourth graders reach proficient or advanced levels, and 56% have not achieved the basic level.
- Only 15% of low-income students reach proficient or advanced levels on the fourth grade NAEP compared to 42% of economically advantaged students.
- Almost twice as many low-income students (54%) perform below basic levels as non-poor students (23%).

In schools across the nation, struggling students must receive intensive instructional support and intervention to catch up quickly. They need SRA's *Corrective Reading*.

* The Education Trust and EdTrust.org

Research Proves Corrective Reading Helps Close the Achievement Gap and Improves Test Scores

Educators are increasingly turning to *Corrective Reading* to deliver the extra support that struggling readers need to succeed. Using the research-based, classroom-proven SRA/McGraw-Hill **Direct Instruction** methodology, this comprehensive intervention program:

- Acts as a scaffold for good teaching behaviors
- Provides a well-organized scope and sequence
- Has coordinated and aligned practice materials and activities
- Includes assessment to help with proper placement and movement of instruction

As with all SRA **Direct Instruction** programs, effective instructional principles are embedded in the program's content so that:

- Skills and strategies are presented explicitly.
- Complex tasks are analyzed and broken down into component parts.
- Each part is taught in a logical progression.
- Brief, frequent practice is provided to ensure mastery of each of the processes and skills.
- Materials are organized to provide cumulative review of skills.
- The amount of new information is controlled and connected to prior learning.
- Consistent lesson formats allow pre-teaching and re-teaching as needed.

To enable educators to make the best use of their time, teacher-friendly instructional routines provide:

- Direct teaching
- Teacher modeling and demonstration
- Guided and independent practice and application with corrective feedback
- Frequent interactions between teacher and students
- Appropriate pacing of lessons
- Adequate practice and review

1. Independent Scientific Research

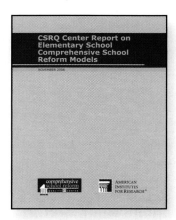

SRA Direct Instruction programs received the highest ranking for program effectiveness in an independent analysis conducted by the *American Institutes for Research* in 2006.

Order #: R80001419

28 studies in peer-reviewed journals show *Corrective Reading* closes the achievement gap for a wide range of students, including students in general education, Title I, Special Education, and alternative settings.

2. Professional Development Validation

A National Reading Panel report on *Teaching Children to Read* and *READING NEXT: A Vision for Action* and *Research in Middle and High School Literacy* **both recommend direct, explicit, comprehensive instruction** as an effective practice, with an emphasis on essential elements appropriate to students' reading development.

3. Results in Real Schools and Classrooms

Corrective Reading **has been proven in classrooms across the nation,** serving children in a wide range of grade levels and socioeconomic and ethnic groups.

Order #: R80001963

Corrective Reading: The Right Components for Comprehensive, Coordinated Intervention

Core Components

Decoding Level	Teacher Presentation Book	Student Book (non-consumable)	Student Workbook (consumable)	Teaching Tutor (Professional Development)
A	✓		✓	✓
B1	✓	✓	✓	✓
B2	✓	✓	✓	✓
C	✓	✓	✓	✓
Comprehension Level				
A/Fast Cycle A	✓		✓	✓
B1/Fast Cycle B1	✓		✓	✓
B2	✓		✓	✓
C	✓	✓	✓	✓

Tools to Differentiate Instruction

Decoding Level	Student Practice CD-ROM	Enrichment Blackline Masters
A	✓	✓
B1	✓	✓
B2	✓	✓
C	✓	✓
Comprehension Level		
A/Fast Cycle A	✓	
B1/Fast Cycle B1	✓	✓
B2	✓	✓
C	✓	✓

Helpful Resources Aligned With Corrective Reading

Decoding Level	Teacher's Resource Book	Content Connections*	Practicing Standardized Test Format (Blackline Masters)	Ravenscourt Books
A	✓	✓	✓	✓
B1	✓	✓	✓	✓
B2	✓	✓	✓	✓
C	✓	✓	✓	✓
Comprehension Level				
A/Fast Cycle A	✓	—	✓	✓
B1/Fast Cycle B1	✓	—	✓	✓
B2	✓	—	✓	✓
C	✓	—	✓	✓

* Used with the Decoding or Comprehension Programs

The ***Corrective Reading*** program provides educators with the tools to help close the achievement gap by addressing deficiencies in both Decoding and Comprehension.

- Two major strands and four instructional levels address a wide range of reading problems.
- Decoding and Comprehension can be used as a supplemental intervention or combined for use as a comprehensive program.
- Multiple points of entry appropriately address skill levels of students in Grades 4–Adult.
- Fully integrated assessments monitor progress and guide movement through the program.

When You Need Decoding Intervention

Students who need Decoding intervention typically have little reading experience and are not familiar with the vocabulary, sentence structure, text organization, and concepts of "book" language. Without intervention, their comprehension skills decline, they develop negative attitudes toward reading, and they become poor spellers and writers.

Students with Decoding problems:

- Make frequent word identification errors
- Add and omit words
- Confuse high-frequency words
- Have a poor grasp of grapheme-phoneme relationships
- Read at a laboriously slow rate
- Are unable to comprehend because of inaccurate reading

When You Need Comprehension Intervention

Students who need Comprehension intervention do not write well, do not think or speak with clarity, and are not highly motivated.

Students with Comprehension problems:

- Cannot follow multi-step directions
- Exhibit poor auditory memory and statement repetition skills
- Lack the analytical skills required to process arguments
- Have a deficient vocabulary
- Lack background or domain knowledge

Decoding A Word-Attack Basics

Decoding A addresses non-readers by teaching sound-spelling relationships. Students quickly develop reading strategies for sounding out words and applying those strategies in context.

Decoding A in Brief

65 Lessons

45 Minutes

Targeted Students: Non-readers or those in Grades 3.5–Adult who read so haltingly they cannot understand what they have read

Outcomes: 60 wpm, 98% accuracy, reading at a 2.0–2.5 grade level

What is Taught

Phonemic Awareness
- Auditory rhyming and pronunciation
- Recognition and production of sounds
- Auditory segmenting
- Auditory blending
- Identifying beginning, ending, and medial sounds

Phonics Skills
- Sound-symbol relationships
- Spelling
- Letter combining
- Blending
- Word reading
  - Regularly spelled words
  - High-utility irregular words
  - High-frequency words
- Reading decodable connected text

Fluency
- Tracking
- Reading within specified rate and accuracy criteria

Comprehension
- Answering oral questions

Corrective Reading Decoding A

Decoding B1 and B2 Decoding Strategies

Decoding B1 and B2 refine word-attack skills by introducing new words and promoting word discrimination. Students build fluency and comprehension by reading stories of increasing length and difficulty.

What is Taught

Phonemic Awareness
- Auditory pronunciation
- Recognition and production of sounds
- Auditory segmenting
- Identifying beginning, ending, and medial sounds

Phonics and Word Analysis
- Sound-symbol relationships with an emphasis on
  - Consonant blends
  - Vowel sounds
  - Letter combinations-Word endings
- Spelling
- Blending
- Word reading
  - Words with consistent orthographic relationships
  - Silent-e words
  - High-utility irregular words
  - High-frequency words
- Daily reading of decodable connected text

Fluency
- Tracking
- Reading and rereading decodable connected text
- Practice for rate and accuracy
- Charting of daily fluency progress

Comprehension
- Story details
- Cause and effect
- Main idea
- Story grammar/retelling
- Story summarizing
- Compare/contrast

Decoding B1 and B2 in Brief

65 Lessons Each

45 Minutes Each

Targeted Students: Poor readers, students in Grades 4–Adult who do not read at an adequate rate and who confuse words

B1 Outcomes: 90 wpm, 98% accuracy, reading at a 3.5–3.9 grade level

B2 Outcomes: 130 wpm, 98% accuracy, reading at a 4.5–4.9 grade level

Corrective Reading Decoding B1 and B2

Decoding C Skill Applications

Decoding C helps students bridge the gap between advanced word-attack skills and the ability to read textbooks and other informational material. Students learn more than 600 new vocabulary words and read a variety of text that prepares them to read in all content areas.

Decoding C in Brief

125 Lessons

45 Minutes

Targeted Students: Grades 6 and up, those readers who lack comprehension of sophisticated text, who do not learn well from what they read, or who have trouble thinking critically

Outcomes: 150 wpm, 98% accuracy, reading at a 6.5–7.0 grade level

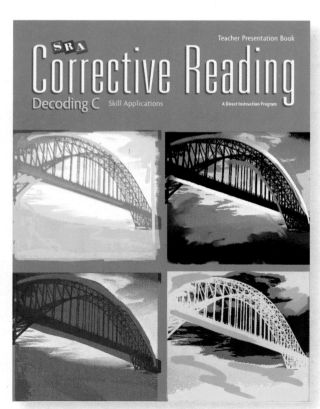

Corrective Reading Decoding C

What is Taught

Phonemic Awareness
- Review of auditory pronunciation, both recognition and production of sounds
- Auditory segmenting
- Identifying beginning, ending, and medial sounds

Phonics and Word Analysis
- Review of letter combinations within words
- Additional sound combinations
- Affixes and their meanings
- Decoding multi-syllabic words using known parts
- Daily reading of decodable connected text
- Reading selections that contain a high percentage of new words
- Reading narrative and expository text

Fluency
- Tracking
- Reading and rereading decodable connected text
- Practice for rate and accuracy
- Charting of daily fluency progress

Comprehension
- Cause and effect
- Main idea
- Compare/contrast
- Sequencing
- Summarizing/retelling
- Referencing text for specific factual information

Comprehension A Thinking Basics

Comprehension A creates a framework for learning new information and filling in background knowledge. Teachers are able to engage students in higher-order thinking skills based on this new foundation of knowledge.

What is Taught

Vocabulary Knowledge
- Definitions of common words
- Synonyms and antonyms
- Descriptions

Logical Thinking Skills
- Deductions
- Statement inferences
- Analogies
- Classification
- Drawing conclusions using basic evidence
- Compare/contrast

Common Semantics
- All/Every
- All/Some/None
- And/Or
- No/Don't

Information and Background Knowledge
- Calendar (months, seasons, holidays)
- Classes of animals
- Practice organizing groups of related facts
- Recitation practice to build auditory memory

Comprehension A in Brief	
Normal Cycle	**Fast Cycle for Middle and High School**
65 Lessons	30 Lessons
45 Minutes	45 Minutes

Targeted Students: Poor comprehenders in Grades 3–Adult who cannot understand much of the material taught at grade level

Outcomes: Higher-order thinking skills and increased vocabulary base

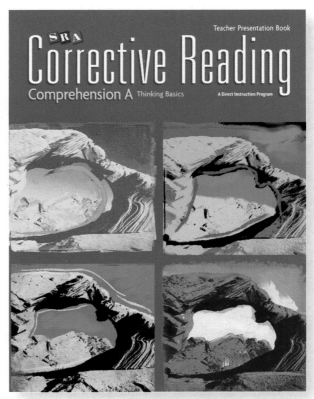

Corrective Reading Comprehension A

Comprehension B1 and B2 Comprehension Skills

Comprehension B1 and B2 develop the skills necessary to construct meaning from content-based text. This enables students to comprehend any subject matter they read and learn new information efficiently.

Comprehension B1 and B2 in Brief	
Normal Cycle	**Fast Cycle for Middle and High School**
B1 – 60 Lessons B2 – 65 Lessons	B1 – 35 Lessons
45 Minutes	45 Minutes

Targeted Students: Poor readers in Grades 4–Adult who have difficulty drawing conclusions, understanding contradictions, and following written directions

Outcomes: Cross-curricular comprehension skills for all subject areas

What is Taught

Vocabulary Knowledge
- Definitions of common words
- Synonyms and antonyms
- Descriptions

Logical Thinking Skills
- Deductions using *some, every, do not*
- Using basic evidence to explain an outcome
- Analogies/similes
- Statement inferences
- Classification
- Identifying contradictions

Sentence/Writing Skills
- Parts of speech
- Subject/predicate
- Combining sentences
- Subject/verb agreement
- Sentence analysis
- Writing step-by-step directions
- Writing paragraphs
- Writing stories
- Editing for word usage, punctuation, redundancy

Information and Background Knowledge
- Names and parts of major body systems *(skeletal, digestive, muscular, circulatory, respiratory, nervous)*
- Organizing groups of related facts
- Rules that explain how body systems work
- Rules that explain why prices change
- Use of deductions to apply rules

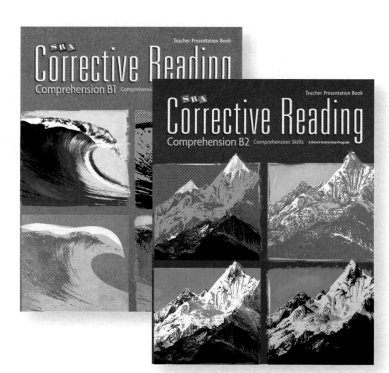

Corrective Reading Comprehension B1 and B2

Comprehension C Concept Applications

Comprehension C helps teachers bridge the gap between basic reasoning and critical thinking. With these skills, students can evaluate and utilize informational resources on their own.

What is Taught

Vocabulary Knowledge
- Definitions
- Meaning from context

Organizing Information
- Main idea/moral
- Outlining
- Making statements more specific or general
- Visual-spatial displays

Logical Thinking Skills
- Deductions
- Using basic evidence to explain a conclusion
- Learning and applying rules of syllogistic reasoning
- Distinguishing between fact and ought statements
- Identifying and explaining contradictions

Using Sources of Information
- Reading for specific factual information
- Determining how they arrive at an answer
- Maps, pictures, graphs
- Recognizing discrepancies
- Choosing appropriate sources (dictionary, atlas, encyclopedia)

Comprehension C in Brief
140 Lessons
45 Minutes
Targeted Students: Grades 6 and up, those readers who lack comprehension of sophisticated text, who do not learn well from what they read, or who have trouble thinking critically
Outcomes: Applying analytical skills to real-life situations and answering inferential versus literal questions based on specific passages read

Corrective Reading Comprehension C

**Corrective Reading
Teaching Tutor CD-ROMs**

Professional Development can be accessed at any time. *SRA Teaching Tutor* CD-ROMs provide ongoing support for teachers using ***Corrective Reading***.

- Directly tied to Decoding or Comprehension
- Feature informative text and classroom examples
- Allow teachers to easily review key formats and teaching techniques
- Easy to access and easy to use

Assessment Materials incorporated in the Teacher Presentation Books provide frequent assessment of student progress.

- Easy-to-use format helps you monitor growth and diagnose potential problems
- Remediation activities provide systematic instruction to address deficient skills

Fast Cycle options for Comprehension A and B1 accelerate student progress.

- Appropriate for older, more advanced students
- Quickly and efficiently covers content from the core program in approximately half as many lessons
- Provides for entry into the core program nearer grade level

Activities Reinforce Skills and Learning at Every Level

Practice and Review Activities—Decoding

Lesson Range	1–15	16–25	26–35	36–45	46–65	66–95	96–125
Level A	• Sound ID • Fooler: Word Lists	• Sound ID • Fooler: Word Lists	• Word ID • Fooler: Sentences	• Word ID • Fooler: Sentences	• Word ID • Fooler: Sentences	• N/A	• N/A
Level B1	• Sound ID • Fooler: Word Lists	• Word ID • Fooler: Sentences	• Word ID • Fooler: Sentences	• Comprehension • Fooler: Sentences	• Comprehension • Fooler: Sentences	• N/A	• N/A
Level B2	• Word ID • Fooler: Sentences	• Word ID • Fooler: Sentences	• Comprehension • Fooler: Sentences	• Comprehension • Fooler: Sentences	• Comprehension • Fooler: Sentences	• N/A	• N/A
Level C	• Vocab: Word Lists • Fooler: Sentences	• N/A • Fooler: Sentences	• N/A • Comprehension	• Vocab: Sentences • Comprehension	• Vocab: Word Lists • Comprehension	• Vocab: Sentences • Comprehension	• Vocab: Sentences • Comprehension

Practice and Review Activities—Comprehension

Lesson Range	1–15	16–25	26–35	36–45	46–65	66–95	96–120	121–140
Level A	• Fact Game	• Fact Game	• Fact Game	• Fact Game	• Fact Game	• N/A	• N/A	• N/A
Level B1	• Fact Game • Vocab: Word Lists	• Fact Game	• Fact Game • Vocab: Word Lists	• Fact Game	• Fact Game • Vocab: Word Lists	• N/A • N/A	• N/A • N/A	• N/A • N/A
Level B2	• Fact Game • Vocab: Word Lists	• Fact Game • N/A	• Fact Game • Vocab: Word Lists	• Fact Game • N/A	• Fact Game • Vocab: Word Lists	• N/A • N/A	• N/A • N/A	• N/A • N/A
Level C	• Fact Game • N/A	• N/A • N/A	• Fact Game • Vocab: Word Lists	• Fact Game • N/A	• Fact Game • N/A	• Fact Game • Vocab: Word Lists	• Fact Game • Vocab: Sentences	• Fact Game • Vocab: Sentences

Corrective Reading Practice Software

Practice Software offers engaging, interactive review to help students master key skills.

- Brief, frequent practice activities and games
- Directly linked to daily lessons
- Allows you to monitor student progress and performance

Bolster Your Corrective Reading Program With These Helpful Support Materials

These additional support materials help teachers build on the skills developed by *Corrective Reading*, further enhancing achievement levels:

Content Connections

- Four books contribute to comprehension with authentic narrative and expository selections read aloud to students.
- Models, techniques, and activities advance active comprehension skills when used with Decoding or Comprehension.
- Reflective and responsive listening activities promote listening skills.
- Graphic organizers emphasize skills to acquire information and build understanding.
- Content connects classroom learning to other subject areas.

Teacher's Resource Books

- Eight books, one for each of four levels in the Decoding and Comprehension strands, make it easy to reinforce and extend daily lessons in *Corrective Reading*.
- *Leveled Passages* offer brief, frequent opportunities for vocabulary and comprehension development.
- Instruction and assessment can be performed congruently.
- *Accommodating All Learners* section contains comprehensive guidance for teachers to help all students acquire key skills and content.
- Efficient remedies address the specific needs of students who have shown reading deficiencies and English learners.
- *Scope and Sequence* helps explain the instructional approach.
- Advanced methodology and tools help teachers ensure students will transfer key skills to the regular curriculum.

Ravenscourt Books Collection

Ravenscourt Collections	For Students Who Have Completed	Reading Level
• *Getting Started* • *Discovery*	Decoding A or Comprehension A	1
• *Anything's Possible* • *The Unexpected*	Decoding B1 or Comprehension B1	2
• *Express Yourself* • *Overcoming Adversity*	Decoding B2 or Comprehension B2	3
• *Moving Forward* • *Reaching Goals*	Decoding C or Comprehension C Lessons 1–60	5

The ***Corrective Reading*** program provides students, teachers, and administrators with all the critical components of a research-based, classroom-proven approach to closing the achievement gap for struggling readers.

Student Benefits

- Age-appropriate materials
- Highly skilled teachers
- Cross-curricular success
- Immediate feedback
- Long-term growth
- Increased achievement

Teacher Benefits

- Coherent, overall instructional design
- Logical organization of materials
- Coordinated instructional sequences
- Specific scaffolding instruction
- Fully aligned student materials
- Classroom management strategies
- Resources for Differentiated Instruction
- Easy-to-access professional development
- Motivated, successful students

Administrator Benefits

- Clearly stated goals and objectives
- Highly qualified teachers
- Instructional efficiency
- Adaptability
- Ongoing assessment and evaluation
- Academic success

Corrective Reading
Comprehension and Decoding
Grades 3–Adult

Response to Intervention

Corrective Reading meets the Response to Intervention requirements of the Individuals with Disabilities Education Act (IDEA).

What Is the

SRA *Teacher's Resource Book?*

The *Teacher's Resource Book* provides resources and materials for extra support for students in the ***Corrective Reading*** program. Materials in this book are divided into five important sections.

1 Ideas for providing **Access Points for Students with Significant Cognitive Disabilities** to allow **all** students a chance to achieve success with the program materials.

2 Tips and suggestions for **Differentiated Instruction** to help you enhance learning for **all** students. Instructional tips provide you with important suggestions to enhance academic success for approaching-mastery, at-mastery, and ELL students. These tips and suggestions align with assessments found in the ***Corrective Reading*** program.

3 A guide to **Professional Development** for Fluency Building and Reading Level Determination provides an overview of fluency as it pertains to ***Corrective Reading*** and a Reading Checkout Chart illustrating number of words per reading checkout, time of checkout, error limits, minimum words correct per minute for reading checkout, and independent/instructional/frustrational reading levels.

4 **Leveled Passages for Comprehension and Vocabulary Practice** designed to assist students with improving their overall comprehension and vocabulary and to allow students to have additional practice applying reading strategies and skills to leveled passages.

5 A **Scope and Sequence Chart** provides an overview of the skills taught in each major component of the program level. In a quick glance, you can see what skills are taught in each piece of the program.

Access Points

for Students
with Significant Cognitive Disabilities

Access Points for Students with Significant Cognitive Disabilities

The following table presents helpful tips for providing access to the **Corrective Reading** curriculum for students with significant cognitive disabilities. These suggestions use foundational skills that are clearly linked to the **Corrective Reading** content to aid such students in achieving academic success. Access points are provided at three levels of instructional complexity to allow all learners the opportunity to experience success in the program materials.

Corrective Reading   Level B2

Independent: The student will:
- blend three to four phonemes to form words;
- decode words with common long and short vowel CVC/CVCe spelling patterns;
- decode phonetically regular CVC, CCVC/CVCC words;
- write 10 or more sounds;
- identify different word endings (-ed, -ing, -s/es);
- recognize high frequency sight words;
- use self-correction;
- read text with high frequency sight words and phonetically regular words with accuracy;
- use new vocabulary that is taught directly;
- categorize key vocabulary and tell how things are the same or different;
- repeat rules when prompted and give 2 examples of each;
- determine word meaning using picture dictionary;
- use strategies to repair comprehension;
- select a variety of fiction and nonfiction materials to listen to or read.

Supported: The student will:
- produce common sounds associated with 10 or more letters;
- blend sounds to decode VC/CVC words;
- recognize high frequency sight words;
- use new vocabulary that is taught directly;
- identify meaning of words paired with pictures;
- repeat rules when prompted;
- relate new vocabulary to prior knowledge;
- listen to and talk about stories;
- identify details such as who, what, and where in text;
- identify words that describe people;
- repeat rules with assistance;
- respond to literal yes/no questions with assistance;
- select and listen to a variety of fiction and nonfiction materials.

Participatory: The student will:
- respond to spoken words/gestures/signs/referent objects/pictures/symbols;
- request continuation of a familiar daily task when it has been interrupted;
- use new vocabulary that is taught directly;
- listen to and respond to stories and informational text;
- match objects/pictures/gestures/signs/symbols to tasks in routines;
- seek assistance with prompting to clarify meaning of pictures/symbols/gestures/signs/words in activities;
- respond to patterns of language in text;
- match make believe pictures in program with real pictures gathered from other sources;
- express a preference for stories;
- identify familiar people/objects/actions by name as stories are read;
- attend to read-aloud fiction and nonfiction materials.

Differentiating Instruction

Recommendations
for Instructional-Level Support

Differentiating Instruction
Decoding B2

Test	Student Level	Tips for Teachers
Mastery Test 1 (After Lesson 10)	Approaching Mastery	• See "Remedies" in *Teacher's Presentation Book* page 77. • Partner with "at mastery" student and review sounds and words; develop flashcards for extra practice. • Re-teach difficult sounds and words using "firming" list. • Review word identification (circling words), word endings, and spelling until firm. • Use "cover-copy-compare" for spelling: Student sees word, covers word, writes word, uncovers model word and compares to word written, and corrects spelling if needed. • Discuss word meanings when appropriate to enhance vocabulary development. • Review comprehension questions; teach student to monitor his or her own comprehension during reading, rereading and slowing down when necessary and asking questions after paragraphs are read. • Review finger placement and tracking for story reading. • Partner with "at mastery" student and have him or her model reading story with prosody; have student read story. • Use paired reading: Good reader reads until student signals for his or her turn to read. • Develop tape of story read by good reader (e.g., "at mastery" student, adult); have student listen to tape and whisper read. • Have student complete *Decoding B2 Enrichment Blackline Masters* and *Practicing Decoding Skills: Standardized Test Format* lessons. • Conduct *Content Connections* lessons to enhance listening comprehension, story reading, and graphic organizer skills. • Conduct "see-say-write:" Student sees sound/word, says sound/word, and writes sound/word until firm.
	At Mastery	• See "Remedies" in *Teacher's Presentation Book* page 77. • Partner with "approaching mastery" or ELL student and review sounds and words; use flashcards for extra practice. • Discuss word meanings when appropriate to enhance vocabulary development. • Review comprehension questions; teach student to monitor his or her own comprehension during reading, rereading and slowing down when necessary and asking questions after paragraphs are read. • Partner with "approaching mastery" or ELL student and model reading story with prosody; have student read story. • Have student tape him or herself reading story as model for "approaching mastery" or ELL student. • Have student complete *Decoding B2 Enrichment Blackline Masters* and *Practicing Decoding Skills: Standardized Test Format* lessons. • Conduct *Content Connections* lessons to enhance listening comprehension, story reading, and graphic organizer skills. • Direct student to reading and writing center in classroom to reinforce literacy and writing skills.

	ELL	• See "Tips for Teachers" for "approaching mastery" and "at mastery" students. • Describe and model mouth formations for difficult sounds and words, then guide student while practicing with mirror. • Have student listen to audiotape and practice saying sounds, words, and sentences with mirror. • Show realia or other visuals of objects (e.g., *files, slides*). • Use gestures (e.g., *stepping*) to demonstrate action words. • Teach cognates when possible to develop comprehension skills (e.g., teach cognate for *firm*). • Use primary language equivalents when available and then ask student to say the words in English.
Mastery Test 2 (After Lesson 20)	Approaching Mastery	• See "Remedies" in *Teacher's Presentation Book* page 135. • Partner with "at mastery" student and review sounds and words; develop flashcards for extra practice. • Re-teach difficult sounds and words using "firming" list. • Review word identification (circling words), word endings, and spelling until firm. • Use "cover-copy-compare" for spelling. • Discuss word meanings when appropriate to enhance vocabulary development. • Review comprehension questions; teach student to monitor his or her own comprehension during reading, rereading and slowing down when necessary and asking questions after paragraphs are read. • Review finger placement and tracking for story reading. • Partner with "at mastery" student and have him or her model reading story with prosody; have student read story. • Use paired reading. • Develop tape of story read by good reader; have student listen to tape and whisper read. • Have student complete *Decoding B2 Enrichment Blackline Masters* and *Practicing Decoding Skills: Standardized Test Format* lessons. • Conduct *Content Connections* lessons to enhance listening comprehension, story reading, and graphic organizer skills. • Conduct "see-say-write."
	At Mastery	• See "Remedies" in *Teacher's Presentation Book* page 135. • Partner with "approaching mastery" or ELL student and review sounds and words; use flashcards for extra practice. • Discuss word meanings when appropriate to enhance vocabulary development. • Review comprehension questions; teach student to monitor his or her own comprehension during reading, rereading and slowing down when necessary and asking questions after paragraphs are read. • Partner with "approaching mastery" or ELL student and model reading story with prosody; have student read story. • Have student tape him or herself reading story as model for "approaching mastery" or ELL student. • Have student complete *Decoding B2 Enrichment Blackline Masters* and *Practicing Decoding Skills: Standardized Test Format* lessons. • Conduct *Content Connections* lessons to enhance listening comprehension, story reading, and graphic organizer skills. • Direct student to reading and writing center in classroom to reinforce literacy and writing skills.

	ELL	• See "Tips for Teachers" for "approaching mastery" and "at mastery" students. • Describe and model mouth formations for difficult sounds and words, then guide student while practicing with mirror. • Have student listen to audiotape and practice saying sounds, words, and sentences with mirror. • Show realia or other visuals of objects. • Use gestures to demonstrate action words. • Use primary language equivalents when available and then ask student to say the words in English.
Mastery Test 3 (After Lesson 30)	Approaching Mastery	• See "Remedies" in *Teacher's Presentation Book* page 189. • Partner with "at mastery" student and review sounds and words; develop flashcards for extra practice. • Re-teach difficult sounds and words using "firming" list. • Review word identification (circling words), word endings, and spelling until firm. • Use "cover-copy-compare" for spelling. • Discuss word meanings when appropriate to enhance vocabulary development. • Review comprehension questions; teach student to monitor his or her own comprehension during reading, rereading and slowing down when necessary and asking questions after paragraphs are read. • Review finger placement and tracking for story reading. • Partner with "at mastery" student and have him or her model reading story with prosody; have student read story. • Use paired reading. • Develop tape of story read by good reader; have student listen to tape and whisper read. • Have student complete *Decoding B2 Enrichment Blackline Masters* and *Practicing Decoding Skills: Standardized Test Format* lessons. • Conduct *Content Connections* lessons to enhance listening comprehension, story reading, and graphic organizer skills. • Conduct "see-say-write."
	At Mastery	• See "Remedies" in *Teacher's Presentation Book* page 189. • Partner with "approaching mastery" or ELL student and review sounds and words; use flashcards for extra practice. • Discuss word meanings when appropriate to enhance vocabulary development. • Review comprehension questions; teach student to monitor his or her own comprehension during reading, rereading and slowing down when necessary and asking questions after paragraphs are read. • Partner with "approaching mastery" or ELL student and model reading story with prosody; have student read story. • Have student tape him or herself reading story as model for "approaching mastery" or ELL student. • Have student complete *Decoding B2 Enrichment Blackline Masters* and *Practicing Decoding Skills: Standardized Test Format* lessons. • Conduct Content Connections lessons to enhance listening comprehension, story reading, and graphic organizer skills. • Direct student to reading and writing center in classroom to reinforce literacy and writing skills.

	ELL	• See "Tips for Teachers" for "approaching mastery" and "at mastery" students.
		• Describe and model mouth formations for difficult sounds and words, then guide student while practicing with mirror.
		• Have student listen to audiotape and practice saying sounds, words, and sentences with mirror.
		• Discuss meanings of sentences where appropriate to enhance comprehension.
		• Teach cognates when possible to develop comprehension skills.
		• Show realia or other visuals of objects.
		• Use Total Physical Response (TPR) to show concepts by saying word or phrase and then demonstrating concept by pantomiming or gesturing (e.g., say, "The wolf pup lay down," then pantomime "lay down," say, "curled up in a little ball," then pantomime, "curled up," say, "quickly fell asleep," then pantomime "fell asleep"); guide student as he or she uses TPR to demonstrate concept.
		• Use gestures to demonstrate action words.
		• Use primary language equivalents when available and then ask student to say the words in English.
Mastery Test 4 (After Lesson 40)	Approaching Mastery	• See "Remedies" in *Teacher's Presentation Book* page 244.
		• Partner with "at mastery" student and review sounds and words; develop flashcards for extra practice.
		• Re-teach difficult sounds and words using "firming" list.
		• Review word identification (circling words), word endings, and spelling until firm.
		• Use "cover-copy-compare" for spelling.
		• Discuss word meanings when appropriate to enhance vocabulary development.
		• Review comprehension questions; teach student to monitor his or her own comprehension during reading, rereading and slowing down when necessary and asking questions after paragraphs are read.
		• Review finger placement and tracking for story reading.
		• Partner with "at mastery" student and have him or her model reading story with prosody; have student read story.
		• Use paired reading.
		• Develop tape of story read by good reader; have student listen to tape and whisper read.
		• Have student complete *Decoding B2 Enrichment Blackline Masters* and *Practicing Decoding Skills: Standardized Test Format* lessons.
		• Conduct *Content Connections* lessons to enhance listening comprehension, story reading, and graphic organizer skills.
		• Conduct "see-say-write."

	At Mastery	• See "Remedies" in *Teacher's Presentation Book* page 244. • Partner with "approaching mastery" or ELL student and review sounds and words; use flashcards for extra practice. • Discuss word meanings when appropriate to enhance vocabulary development. • Review comprehension questions; teach student to monitor his or her own comprehension during reading, rereading and slowing down when necessary and asking questions after paragraphs are read. • Partner with "approaching mastery" or ELL student and model reading story with prosody; have student read story. • Have student tape him or herself reading story as model for "approaching mastery" or ELL student. • Have student complete *Decoding B2 Enrichment Blackline Masters* and *Practicing Decoding Skills: Standardized Test Format* lessons. • Conduct *Content Connections* lessons to enhance listening comprehension, story reading, and graphic organizer skills. • Direct student to reading and writing center in classroom to reinforce literacy and writing skills.
	ELL	• See "Tips for Teachers" for "approaching mastery" and "at mastery" students. • Describe and model mouth formations for difficult sounds and words, then guide student while practicing with mirror. • Have student listen to audiotape and practice saying sounds, words, and sentences with mirror. • Teach cognates when possible to develop comprehension skills. • Show realia or other visuals of objects. • Use TPR to show concepts by saying word or phrase and then demonstrating concept by pantomiming or gesturing; guide student as he or she uses TPR to demonstrate concept. • Use gestures to demonstrate action words. • Use primary language equivalents when available and then ask student to say the words in English.
Mastery Test 5 (After Lesson 50)	Approaching Mastery	• See "Remedies" in *Teacher's Presentation Book* page 301. • Partner with "at mastery" student and review sounds and words; develop flashcards for extra practice. • Re-teach difficult sounds and words using "firming" list. • Review word identification (circling words), word endings, and spelling until firm. • Use "cover-copy-compare" for spelling. • Discuss word meanings when appropriate to enhance vocabulary development. • Review comprehension questions; teach student to monitor his or her own comprehension during reading, rereading and slowing down when necessary and asking questions after paragraphs are read. • Review finger placement and tracking for story reading. • Partner with "at mastery" student and have him or her model reading story with prosody; have student read story. • Use paired reading. • Develop tape of story read by good reader; have student listen to tape and whisper read. • Have student complete *Decoding B2 Enrichment Blackline Masters* and *Practicing Decoding Skills: Standardized Test Format* lessons. • Conduct *Content Connections* lessons to enhance listening comprehension, story reading, and graphic organizer skills. • Conduct "see-say-write."

	At Mastery	• See "Remedies" in *Teacher's Presentation Book* page 301. • Partner with "approaching mastery" or ELL student and review sounds and words; use flashcards for extra practice. • Discuss word meanings when appropriate to enhance vocabulary development. • Review comprehension questions; teach student to monitor his or her own comprehension during reading, rereading and slowing down when necessary and asking questions after paragraphs are read. • Partner with "approaching mastery" or ELL student and model reading story with prosody; have student read story. • Have student tape him or herself reading story as model for "approaching mastery" or ELL student. • Have student complete *Decoding B2 Enrichment Blackline Masters* and *Practicing Decoding Skills: Standardized Test Format* lessons. • Conduct *Content Connections* lessons to enhance listening comprehension, story reading, and graphic organizer skills. • Direct student to reading and writing center in classroom to reinforce literacy and writing skills.
	ELL	• See "Tips for Teachers" for "approaching mastery" and "at mastery" students. • Describe and model mouth formations for difficult sounds and words, then guide student while practicing with mirror. • Have student listen to audiotape and practice saying sounds, words, and sentences with mirror. • Show realia or other visuals of objects. • Use TPR to show concepts by saying word or phrase and then demonstrating concept by pantomiming or gesturing; guide student as he or she uses TPR to demonstrate concept. • Use gestures to demonstrate action words. • Use primary language equivalents when available and then ask student to say the words in English.
Mastery Test 6 (End-of-Program)	Approaching Mastery	• See "Remedies" in *Teacher's Presentation Book* page 391. • Partner with "at mastery" student and review sounds and words; develop flashcards for extra practice. • Re-teach difficult sounds and words using "firming" list. • Review word endings and spelling until firm. • Use "cover-copy-compare" for spelling. • Discuss word meanings when appropriate to enhance vocabulary development. • Review comprehension questions; teach student to monitor his or her own comprehension during reading, rereading and slowing down when necessary and asking questions after paragraphs are read. • Review finger placement and tracking for story reading. • Partner with "at mastery" student and have him or her model reading story with prosody; have student read story. • Use paired reading. • Develop tape of story read by good reader; have student listen to tape and whisper read. • Have student complete *Decoding B2 Enrichment Blackline Masters* and *Practicing Decoding Skills: Standardized Test Format* lessons. • Conduct *Content Connections* lessons to enhance listening comprehension, story reading, and graphic organizer skills. • Conduct "see-say-write."

	At Mastery	• See "Remedies" in *Teacher's Presentation Book* page 391.
		• Partner with "approaching mastery" or ELL student and review sounds and words; use flashcards for extra practice.
		• Discuss word meanings when appropriate to enhance vocabulary development.
		• Review comprehension questions; teach student to monitor his or her own comprehension during reading, rereading and slowing down when necessary and asking questions after paragraphs are read.
		• Partner with "approaching mastery" or ELL student and model reading story with prosody; have student read story.
		• Have student tape him or herself reading story as model for "approaching mastery" or ELL student.
		• Have student complete *Decoding B2 Enrichment Blackline Masters* and *Practicing Decoding Skills: Standardized Test Format* lessons.
		• Conduct *Content Connections* lessons to enhance listening comprehension, story reading, and graphic organizer skills.
		• Direct student to reading and writing center in classroom to reinforce literacy and writing skills.
	ELL	• See "Tips for Teachers" for "approaching mastery" and "at mastery" students.
		• Describe and model mouth formations for difficult sounds and words, then guide student while practicing with mirror.
		• Have student listen to audiotape and practice saying sounds, words, and sentences with mirror.
		• Discuss meanings of sentences where appropriate to enhance comprehension.
		• Teach cognates when possible to develop comprehension skills.
		• Show realia or other visuals of objects.
		• Use TPR to show concepts by saying word or phrase and then demonstrating concept by pantomiming or gesturing; guide student as he or she uses TPR to demonstrate concept.
		• Use gestures to demonstrate action words.
		• Use primary language equivalents when available and then ask student to say the words in English.

Professional Development

**Fluency Building
and Reading Level Determination**

Professional Development
Corrective Reading Decoding Levels A, B1, B2, and C
Fluency Building and Reading Level Determination

What is Fluency Building?

Fluency is the ability to read text quickly, accurately, and with expression (Armbruster et al., 2003; Hasbrouck, 2006; NICHD, 2000). It goes beyond automaticity or fast, effortless reading, to include prosody or reading with expression as a critical aspect. Students who know how to read fluently read text smoothly with few, if any, decoding errors; they also read with proper expression, placing vocal emphasis and inflection where needed in the text (e.g., dialogue, punctuation, key words).

Why Fluency Building?

Fluency building is critical because "it provides a bridge between word recognition and comprehension. Because fluent readers do not have to concentrate on decoding the words, they can focus their attention on what the text means. They can make connections among the ideas in the text and between the text and their background knowledge" (Armbruster et al., 2003, p. 22).

Hasbrouck (2006) noted, "When children read too slowly or haltingly, the text devolves into a broken string of words and/or phrases; it's a struggle just to remember what's been read, much less extract its meaning" (p. 24). Thus, programs should focus on building fluency so that reading with understanding is more easily achieved. **Corrective Reading Decoding** includes fluency practice as a key aspect of the program.

Does Oral Reading Fluency Occur in the Corrective Reading Program?

Yes. The **Corrective Reading Decoding** program includes Fluency Assessments—Individual reading checkouts. These checkouts are timed and are 45 seconds (Level A), 1 minute (Levels A, B1, and B2), or 2 minutes (Level C) in duration.

To build fluency, you will have students reread the story of the day one to two more times with a partner following the regular lesson. This rereading is done orally; repeated oral reading has been shown to substantially improve reading fluency and overall reading achievement (Armbruster et al., 2003; Hasbrouck, 2006; NICHD, 2000). Oral reading with a partner is a key part of the **Corrective Reading Decoding** program and takes no more than 6 minutes of instructional time, with long-lasting results. Further, fluency-building activities are extensions of the individual reading checkouts already found in the **Corrective Reading Decoding** program.

What are Accurate Descriptions of Independent, Instructional, and Frustrational Reading Levels for Individual Students?

"Fluency develops as a result of many opportunities to practice reading with a high degree of success. Therefore, your students should practice orally rereading text that is reasonably easy for them" (Armbruster et al., 2003, p. 27). Students can encounter three types of text (Katz, Polkoff, & Gurvitz, 2005; Osborn, Lehr, & Hiebert, 2003):

- Independent level text (relatively easy for the reader, with no more than approximately 1 in 20 words difficult for the reader; 95% success or higher; with 90% comprehension).

- Instructional level text (challenging but manageable text for the reader, with no more than approximately 1 in 10 words difficult for the reader; 90% to 94% success; with 75% comprehension).

- Frustrational level text (problematic text for the reader, with more than 1 in 10 words difficult for the reader; less than 90% success; with 50% comprehension).

- Most researchers advocate the use of text containing words students know or can decode easily (e.g., Allington, 2002; Armbruster et al., 2003; Hasbrouck, 2006). You can determine if a story or text is appropriate for students to read independently using the following steps:

  1 Select a 100–200 word passage from a book that the student has not read previously.

  2 Have the student read the passage aloud. Make sure you start at the beginning of a paragraph and avoid lots of dialogue. Count substitutions, mispronunciations, omissions, reversals, and hesitations for more than 3 seconds as errors; insertions, self corrects, and repetitions do not count as errors.

  3 Subtract the number of errors the student made from the total number of words— this will yield the number of correct words read by the student; divide the number of correct words read by the total number of words in the passage and multiply by 100.

  Example: passage length = 200 words; student makes 12 errors or reads 188 correct words; divide 188 correct words by 200 total words equaling .94; multiply .94 by 100 to get 94%.

  4 Compare the student's calculated accuracy level to the reading level percentages (i.e., 95% or higher = independent level; 90%–94% = instructional; below 90% = frustrational); in the above example, the student would be at an instructional reading level (94% falls in the 90% to 94% range).

  5 Develop 5–8 comprehension questions (at least one "who, what, where, why, and inference-type" question). Ask these comprehension questions after the student reads the passage.

  6 Record each correctly answered question. Subtract the number of questions answered incorrectly from the total number of questions; divide the number of correctly answered questions by the total number of questions and multiply by 100.

Example: number of questions = 6; student answers 1 incorrectly or answers 5 questions correctly; divide 5 correctly answered questions by 6 total questions equaling .83; multiply .83 by 100 to get 83%.

7 Compare the student's calculated percentage correct to the comprehension levels (i.e., 90% = independent; 75% = instructional; 50% = frustrational); in the above example, the student would be at an instructional level (83% is above 75% and less than 90%).

How Can You tell if Students are Working at the Appropriate Instructional Level in the *Corrective Reading Decoding* Program?

The **Corrective Reading Decoding** program is designed with student success in mind.

■ Only a small amount of new learning (10%–15% of the total lesson) occurs in each lesson.

■ New concepts and skills are presented in two or three consecutive lessons to provide students with enough exposure to new material to use it in other applications.

■ The majority of each lesson firms and reviews material and skills presented earlier in the program.

The small-step design of the program promises successful learning for students who are placed appropriately. Four criteria help you determine if students are working at the appropriate instructional level during lessons (Engelmann,1999).

1 Each time a task is presented, the group either responds correctly (all students respond correctly and in unison) or incorrectly (some students give the wrong response, no response, or do not respond in unison). Students should be at least 70% correct on information that is being introduced for the first time. If students are much below 70%, they will find it difficult to learn the skills being presented. If they are only at 50%, they are at chance levels and are probably guessing.

2 Students should be at least 90% correct on parts of the lesson that deal with skills and information taught earlier in the program (assuming previous skill mastery). For example, when students read a passage, they should read at least 90% of the words correct on the first reading because virtually all of the words should be familiar. If students are consistently below the 90% correct level, the amount of new learning is too great.

3 At the end of a lesson, all students should be "virtually 100% firm on all tasks and activities" (p. 6). For example, on the second reading of the passage, students should read with close to 100% accuracy.

4 Students should be at least 85% correct on independent work.

To determine student-reading level, you should complete the reading checkout and words correct per minute (WCPM) calculation as scripted. **Corrective Reading** Checkout Charts provide lesson numbers; number of words per checkout or reading checkout goals; error thresholds; minimum correct words per minute; and independent, instructional, and frustrational reading levels including words correct per minute. These charts are shown on page 24.

You can compare your student's WCPM to the 2005 Hasbrouck and Tindal Oral Reading Fluency Data Chart (see *How do You Help Readers who Struggle with Fluency?* on the next page) to establish who is in need of additional fluency practice.

How Can You Help Students Select Appropriate Material to Read for Personal Pleasure?

Independent reading is the key to success of a life-long reader (Katz et al., 2005). Scaffolded independent reading should be done daily in the classroom; up to 30 minutes of independent reading time is advocated. Scaffolded independent reading involves opportunities for pleasurable, student-selected reading.

To accomplish this scaffolded independent reading, students should be taught a good way to self-select books that are "just right" for their independent reading level. The "Five Finger Rule" helps students determine if books are "too easy," "too hard," or "just right." (Routman, 2003). Students may use the steps below to choose an independent-level book:

1. Choose a book
2. Open it anywhere
3. Make a fist
4. Read the page and hold up one finger for every unknown word or mistake you come across
5. Determine book "level:" 0–1 mistakes = too easy; 2–3 mistakes = just right; 4 or more mistakes = too hard.

How should a Fluency Building Lesson be Conducted?

You should assign student partners for the fluency building activity. These partners can be the same ones used during the individual reading checkouts. To ensure success, students should be matched as closely as possible both in terms of their reading levels and their fluency rates. Given the emphasis on placement testing and flexible skill grouping in the *Corrective Reading Decoding* program, this matching should be relatively easy to accomplish.

Next, you should introduce and teach students how to conduct fluency practice properly in the classroom; this training should be conducted over 1 week. Even after training, you should carefully monitor student pairs during fluency practice activities. The following table overviews what should be taught and how to teach it. If students struggle with fluency goals even after partner reading, they can be encouraged to repeat fluency practice with their partners (Note: Armbruster et al., 2003 report up to four repeated reads of the same passage may be needed to build fluency); however, if students continue to struggle, fluency intervention may be needed (see "*How do You Help Readers who Struggle with Fluency*" on the next page).

What to Teach	How to Teach It
Importance of fluency	• Discuss why fluent reading is important.
Fluency partnership behavior	• Discuss how to treat others (e.g., no arguing, be positive). • Set rules/expectations.
Fluency practice procedure	• Model and practice how/where to sit (across from one another in desks or at table; side by side in desks or at table). • Model and practice set up (one student gets own student book, one student has copy of student book story on which to record errors/last word read). • Model and practice what errors are (unknown/incorrect words). • Model and practice partner reading procedure (teacher times all students for specified time noted in program; recording partners underline unknown/incorrect words and draw slash after last word read when timer sounds; following timing, recording partners go over errors and follow standard error correct procedure [i.e., "That word is brother. What word?"]; recording partners record last word read, number of errors, calculate WPM [correct words per minute] and errors, and graph partners' data on Individual Reading Progress Charts; student roles are reversed and same procedure is followed).

How do You Help Readers who Struggle with Fluency?

Hasbrouck and Tindal (2006) completed an extensive study of oral reading fluency. They recommended using the 2005 Hasbrouck and Tindal Oral Reading Fluency Data Chart (see page 22) to establish who is in need of additional fluency practice beyond that accomplished by partner reading in the classroom. Students scoring below the 50th percentile using an average of two unpracticed readings from grade-level materials need a regimented fluency-building intervention. Additionally, teachers can use the chart to establish long-range goals for students or "aim lines" that can appear on graphs as a visual aid for students.

Students scoring at the frustrational reading level may be an indication of the following:

■ A failure to achieve 70% correct on new information, 90% on skills taught earlier in the program, and virtually 100% on all tasks/activities by the end of a lesson—further training on the program may be warranted.

■ Program placement that is too high—re-administer placement test to ensure appropriate program placement.

■ Double-dosing or completing lesson a second time to ensure skill mastery—once students are above the 90% accuracy level, they can participate more successfully in fluency building activities; fluency building should occur on independent level text although some researchers advocate the use of independent or instructional level text (see Osborn et al., 2003 for details).

Several research–validated strategies can be used to improve fluency.

Problem	Fluency Strategy	How to Do It
Reading without prosody.	Teacher modeling of prosody (echo reading).	Teacher reads story with prosody; approaching mastery student tracks as teacher models prosody; teacher provides guided practice on reading with prosody; sentences or paragraphs can be alternated between teacher and student.
	Tape-assisted modeling of prosody.	Approaching mastery student listens to audiotape of story read with prosody; student whisper reads and tracks as audiotape is played a second time.
	Tutoring.	At-mastery student paired with approaching mastery student; at-mastery student reads, modeling prosody; at-mastery student provides guided practice on reading with prosody.
Failure to meet individual reading checkout goals or score below 50% percentile on Hasbrouck and Tindal (2006) fluency data chart.	Choral reading.	Teacher models reading at appropriate pace; approaching mastery students then read along with teacher at appropriate pace.
	Student-adult reading.	Adult reads story first, modeling appropriate pace (and prosody); approaching mastery student reads same story with adult providing assistance as needed.
	Tape-assisted reading.	Approaching mastery student listens to audiotape of story read at appropriate pace; student whisper reads and tracks as audiotape is played a second time.
	Paired or tandem reading.	At-mastery student is paired with an approaching mastery student; at-mastery student reads along with approaching mastery student at appropriate pace noting, "whenever you want to read alone, just tap the back of my hand"); at-mastery student fades him/herself from reading as approaching mastery student reads more and more of story.

Problem	Fluency Strategy	How to Do It
Errors occur on particular words.	Error word drill.	At end of fluency building session, teacher records all "error" words on whiteboard or index cards; approaching mastery student reviews cards 3–4 times with teacher.
	Reading racetrack.	Teacher records troublesome words on "track segments" forming a racetrack; approaching mastery student points to words on racetrack and reads them for 1 minute, circling the track as many times as possible (Falk, Band, & McLaughlin, 2003).
	Firming list.	Teacher writes troublesome words on board; teacher practices words on daily basis; teacher removes words that are stated correctly 3 sessions in a row.
	Cloze reading.	Teacher models reading at appropriate pace; once or twice every few sentences, teacher omits important words and approaching mastery students read words aloud in choral fashion.

Hasbrouck & Tindal Oral Reading Fluency Data

Jan Hasbrouck and Gerald Tindal completed an extensive study of oral reading fluency in 2004. The results of their study are published in a technical report entitled, "Oral Reading Fluency: 90 Years of Measurement," which is available on the University of Oregon's website, brt.uoregon.edu/tech_reports.htm and in THE READING TEACHER volume 59, 2006.

This table shows the oral reading fluency rates of students in grades 1 through 8 as determined by Hasbrouck and Tindal's data.

You can use the information in this table to draw conclusions and make decisions about the oral reading fluency of your students. **Students scoring below the 50th percentile using the average score of two unpracticed readings from grade-level materials need a fluency-building program.** In addition, teachers can use the table to set the long-term fluency goals for their struggling readers.

Average weekly improvement is the average words per week growth you can expect from a student. It was calculated by subtracting the fall score from the spring score and dividing the difference by 32, the typical number of weeks between the fall and spring assessments. For grade 1, since there is no fall assessment, the average weekly improvement was calculated by subtracting the winter score from the spring score and dividing the difference by 16, the typical number of weeks between the winter and spring assessments.

Grade	Percentile	Fall WCPM*	Winter WCPM*	Spring WCPM*	Avg. Weekly Improvement**
1	90		81	111	1.9
	75		47	82	2.2
	50		23	53	1.9
	25		12	28	1.0
	10		6	15	0.6
2	90	106	125	142	1.1
	75	79	100	117	1.2
	50	51	72	89	1.2
	25	25	42	61	1.1
	10	11	18	31	0.6
3	90	128	146	162	1.1
	75	99	120	137	1.2
	50	71	92	107	1.1
	25	44	62	78	1.1
	10	21	36	48	0.8
4	90	145	166	180	1.1
	75	119	139	152	1.0
	50	94	112	123	0.9
	25	68	87	98	0.9
	10	45	61	72	0.8
5	90	166	182	194	0.9
	75	139	156	168	0.9
	50	110	127	139	0.9
	25	85	99	109	0.8
	10	61	74	83	0.7
6	90	177	195	204	0.8
	75	153	167	177	0.8
	50	127	140	150	0.7
	25	98	111	122	0.8
	10	68	82	93	0.8
7	90	180	192	202	0.7
	75	156	165	177	0.7
	50	128	136	150	0.7
	25	102	109	123	0.7
	10	79	88	98	0.6
8	90	185	199	199	0.4
	75	161	173	177	0.5
	50	133	146	151	0.6
	25	106	115	124	0.6
	10	77	84	97	0.6

*WCPM = Words Correct Per Minute

**Average words per week growth

References

Allington, R. L. (2002). What I've learned about effective reading instruction from a decade of studying exemplary elementary classroom teachers. *Phi Delta Kappan, 83,* 740–747.

Armbruster, B., Lehr, F., & Osborn, J. (2003). *Put reading first: The research building blocks of reading instruction: Grades K–3* (2nd ed.). Washington, DC: Center for the Improvement of Early Reading Achievement, National Institute for Literacy, U.S. Department of Education.

Carnine, D. W., Silbert, J., Kame'enui, E. J., & Tarver, S. G. (2004). Direct Instruction reading (4th ed.). Upper Saddle River, NJ: Pearson Education.

Engelmann, S. (1999, July). *Student-program alignment and teaching to mastery.* Paper presented at the 25th National Direct Instruction Conference, Eugene, OR.

Falk, M., Band, M., & McLaughlin, T. F. (2003). The effects of reading racetracks and flashcards on sight word vocabulary of three third grade students with a specific learning disability: A further replication and analysis. *International Journal of Special Education, 18*(2), 57–61.

Hasbrouck, J. (2006). Drop everything and read—but how?: For students who are not yet fluent, silent reading is not the best use of classroom time. *American Educator, 30*(2), 22–27, 30–31, 46–47.

Hasbrouck, J., & Tindal, G. A. (2006). ORF norms: A valuable assessment tool for reading teachers. *The Reading Teacher, 59,* 636–644.

Katz, C. A., Polkoff, L., & Gurvitz, D. (2005, January). "Shhh...I'm reading:" Scaffolded independent-level reading. *School Talk.* Urbana, IL: National Council of Teachers of English.

National Institute of Child Health and Human Development [NICHD]. (2000). *Report of the National Reading Panel. Teaching children to read: An evidence-based assessment of the scientific research literature on reading and its implications for reading instruction: Reports of the subgroups* (NIH Publication NO. 00–4754). Washington, DC: U.S. Government Printing Office.

Osborn, J., Lehr, F., & Hiebert, E. (2003). *A focus on fluency.* Honolulu, HI: Pacific Resources for Education and Learning.

Routman, R. (2003). *Reading essentials:* The specifics you need to teach reading well. Portsmouth, NH: Heineman.

Vaughn, S., & Linan-Thompson, S. (2004). *Research–based methods of reading instruction: Grades K–3.* Alexandria, VA: ASCD.

Corrective Reading Decoding Level B2 Reading Checkout Chart

Lesson Number	Reading Checkout Goal (Number of Words)	Time (min)	Error Threshold for Passing (No more than)	Minimum Words Correct per Minute	Reading Level					
					Independent[1]		Instructional[1]		Frustrational[1]	
					95% or higher of total words	WCPM	90% to 94% of total words	WCPM	Below 90% of total words	WCPM
2–10	90	1	3	87	≥ 86	≥ 86	81–85	81–85	≤ 80	≤ 80
11–20	100	1	3	97	≥ 95	≥ 95	90–94	90–94	≤ 89	≤ 89
21–40	105	1	3	102	≥ 100	≥ 100	94–99	94–99	≤ 93	≤ 93
41–50	110	1	3	107	≥ 104	≥ 104	99–103	99–103	≤ 98	≤ 98
51–60	120	1	3	117	≥ 114	≥ 114	108–113	108–113	≤ 107	≤ 107
61–65	130	1	3	127	≥ 123	≥ 123	117–122	117–122	≤ 116	≤ 116

[1]Reading level rounded to the nearest percentage.

Leveled Passages

Blackline Masters for Comprehension and Vocabulary Practice

Leveled Passages are aligned with the content in **Corrective Reading** Decoding B2 to provide additional independent practice for students. The following chart presents a lesson correlation for each of the passages.

Leveled Passage	Lesson
The Homework Handshake	5
How Is the Weather?	5
Follow Your Nose, Dog!	10
Watch That Melon	10
Rodney, the Inventor Who Never Gave Up	15
The Red Kangaroo	15
Fit Body, Fit Mind	20
Lady Baseball	20
A New Start	25
Making a Difference	25
Horses of America	30
The Case of the Missing Bear	30
Antarctica	35
Sledding with Grandpa	35
Carl's Summer on the Farm	40
Thomas Edison	40
The Planets in our Solar System	45
Beachcombing	45
At Work in the Forest	50
The Lion and the Mouse	50
The Music of Life	55
Gabby Learns a Lesson	55
A Family Story	60
Animal Helpers	60
A History of Flight	65
Going to America in 1898	65

Leveled Passages for Comprehension and Vocabulary Practice

The following reading selections are designed to assist students with improving their overall comprehension and vocabulary and to allow students to have additional practice applying reading strategies and skills to leveled passages. The blackline masters contain both fiction and non-fiction selections that allow students to practice skills and strategies with a wide range of material. The selections are

- built to provide students with additional opportunities to read independently.

- designed to provide frequent opportunities for application of comprehension strategies and practice with vocabulary skills.

- sequenced to challenge students as they grow throughout the year.

These selections are intended to be used as a supplement to the main reading lesson, and they should not be used instead of the main instructional materials. Students should be able to work through these independently as they build comprehension and reading skills in the core materials. Challenging and unfamiliar words are presented in an outline box. Words contained in these boxes are not easily decodable and may have definitions with which the students may not be familiar. The teacher should pronounce each of these words with students and ensure they have a general understanding of each word's meaning before they begin reading.

Following each reading selection are questions that provide additional practice. These activities fall into one of the following two categories:

- **Comprehension Activities** may be either multiple choice or short answer. Multiple choice questions contain two to three possible answers, and students should select the best answer according to the reading selection. Short answer activities, on the other hand, allow students to provide their own answers. Students may be asked to draw a picture to show what they understand from the selection or put events from the story in chronological order.

- **Learn About Words** activities vary from selection to selection. Students may be asked to find synonyms or antonyms in the selection. Other examples of these activities require students to apply something they already know to material discussed in the reading selection. Students may be asked to circle the correct verb form in a given sentence or deduce a word's meaning from its context or parts.

| Eric | Hmm | Jenna | Marcus |

The Homework Handshake

"Up high, down low, slap me five, way to go," Jeff, Kate, and Eric cheered as they moved their arms and hands up, down, and around in a handshake.

"What are you doing?" Jenna asked. They were in line at the beginning of the school day.

"You always do that handshake," Marcus said.

"Not every day," Eric said. "You'll see. One day you'll get it." Some kids leaned in, hoping Eric would say more. Even their teacher, Mrs. Green, looked at Eric. But Eric didn't say anything else.

As they put their homework in the basket, Jeff, Kate, and Eric smiled. Jenna saw them. "Hmm," she said.

The next day, only Jeff and Eric did the handshake in line. When they turned in their homework, Kate said, "I lost mine."

"Hmm," Jenna said again.

The day after, Jenna slipped into line behind Jeff, Kate, and Eric and said, "I did my homework!" They all did the handshake.

Two days later, Marcus got it. By the end of the week, everybody was doing the handshake, but not Mrs. Green.

For two weeks, they all turned in their homework and did the handshake. Mrs. Green was proud, but she didn't understand. Then one day, Mrs. Green put something in the homework basket. She said, "Can I do the homework handshake, too?"

"You turned in homework, Mrs. Green," Jeff said, "and you got it! You can do the homework handshake, too."

The Homework Handshake 27

The Homework Handshake (continued)

Comprehension Activity

Write the answers to the questions on the lines.

1 Who are the first three students to do the handshake?

_____

2 What does the handshake mean?

_____

_____

3 Why is Mrs. Green proud?

_____

_____

_____

4 How do you know that Mrs. Green understands the homework handshake?

_____

_____

5 Does this story take place at school or at home? How do you know?

_____

_____

_____

Name _____ Date _____

above   weather

How Is the Weather?

What do you see and feel outside? Is it sunny or raining? Is it hot or cold? Do you know why the weather is different each day?

The air and the ground are heated by the sun. Clouds and gas in the sky trap heat, and that keeps us from getting too cold.

Clouds play a big part in making the weather. Clouds hold in heat at night, make shade by day, and bring us rain and snow. When a cloud holds a lot of water, the water turns into rain. If the air is very cold, the rain may freeze into ice or snow. Can you tell when a cloud is holding a lot of water?

Wind moves weather from one spot to another. Hot air moves up, leaving a space below it, and colder air moves into the space. As hot and cold air move around, they make wind. Wind may blow us hot weather or cold weather.

Wind also moves waves of water from one spot to another. If the water is hot, it heats the air above it and makes the weather hotter. If the water is cold, it cools the air above it and makes the weather colder. When wind moves the waves in the sea, they can bring hot or cold weather to places all around the world.

Waves, sun, wind, and clouds work together to make weather. When you go outside, think about everything that makes the weather what it is!

Comprehension Activities

Write the answers to the questions on the lines.

1 What are three ways clouds make the weather different?

_____

_____

_____

How Is the Weather? **29**

How Is the Weather (continued)

2 What are two ways the wind moves weather from one spot to another?

_____

_____

_____

_____

Draw pictures to answer the questions. You may have some words in your pictures.

3 How does heat get to the ground and the air? Draw a picture to show your answer.

4 What happens when hot air moves up? Draw a picture to show your answer.

Name _____ Date _____

cancer	doctors	follow	keen	police	scent

Follow Your Nose, Dog!

If you know dogs, you know they like to follow their noses. They sniff anything from the people they meet to anything on the street. Dogs do this because they have a very good sense of smell. Dogs can smell many times better than people can!

For years, people have used dogs' keen sense of smell to help them. Police use trained dogs to help fight crime and to find things. A dog's nose can track, or follow, the scent of people. They can help the police find people who do not follow the law or people who are missing or trapped.

Dogs can be trained to sniff out some kinds of cancer. These trained dogs use their sense of smell to tell the difference between skin with cancer and skin without cancer. This helps doctors to take care of people so the people can get better. These dogs can help save many lives.

No matter what their job, dogs are trained in much the same way. Often, they find out how to do their job by playing. The trainer throws a rag, and the dog brings it back. Then the trainer adds a smell to the rag. The dog must use its nose to find the rag. After the dog finds that smell, the trainer hides things with the same smell. The dog gets a treat each time it finds the right smell.

Dogs are called "man's best friend." It is good to know their noses can help us!

Follow Your Nose, Dog! 31

Follow Your Nose, Dog! (continued)

Comprehension Activity

Write your answers to the questions on the lines.

1 Name two jobs dogs can do.

_____

2 Why are dogs better at some jobs than people are?

_____

3 In a few sentences, explain how dogs can be trained.

_____

_____

_____

_____

4 What other job do you think a dog might be trained to do? Tell why a dog's sense of smell would help

it do that job.

_____

_____

fence	Harry	melon	Willa

Watch That Melon

Willa and her little brother Harry ran to the garden. They could not wait to see if the melons in their garden were ready to eat.

Willa stepped over the fence and then lifted Harry into the garden. "Look!" Willa said. Under the green leaves was a melon! Willa bent down to look closer and saw three bites in the melon. Willa called to her dad. "Look, Dad. Something has eaten our melon!"

"How could an animal get into the garden? We have this fence," Dad said when he saw the melon.

"We will stop whoever is doing this," Willa said. She looked at three more little melons with small bites. "I'll watch them all day!"

Willa and Harry took turns watching the melons. How slowly they were growing! Still, each day, the melons got a little bigger. As Willa and Harry watched the plants, they saw a toad inside the fence, and they saw bugs on the leaves, but they didn't see anything that could eat their melons.

Then one morning, Willa saw something hop in the grass outside the garden. A rabbit moved closer to the fence, found a hole, and slipped under it. It was going to eat their melons. "Mom, Dad, Harry," Willa yelled. "Come see this!"

They all came running. Mom got to the fence just in time to see the rabbit hop away. "Oh, no you don't," Mom said.

"I'll make a better fence," said Dad, and he fixed all the holes.

When the fence was fixed, there were no more rabbits in the garden. When the leaves turned brown, the melons were ready. Willa picked the biggest melon. "Now we can be the ones to eat the melons." It was the best melon Willa, Harry, Dad, and Mom had ever eaten!

Watch That Melon **33**

Watch That Melon (continued)

Comprehension Activities

Write the answers to the questions on the lines.

1 What is the problem for the family in this story?

_____

_____

2 How is the problem in the story solved?

_____

_____

_____

3 What kinds of animals do Willa and Harry see in and around their garden?

_____

4 Put the events of the story in order by writing 1, 2, 3 and 4.

_____ Willa and Harry take turns watching the melons.

_____ Willa's family eats the melon

_____ Willa sees the rabbit.

_____ Willa finds a melon with bites in it.

grade	invention	inventor	tubes	Rodney

Rodney, the Inventor Who Never Gave Up

Rodney was an inventor. His newest invention was a backpack on wheels. It had a motor and moved by itself. It carried his books, pens, paper, and lunch. Rodney was sure that everybody in his third-grade class would want one.

But things didn't turn out like he'd planned. When Rodney took his backpack invention to school, it was a big mess. It bumped into students. It crashed into his teacher.

"Stop that thing!" called his teacher, Ms. Green.

Rodney picked up his backpack. "A good inventor never gives up," he said. "And I, Rodney, will never give up."

Soon Rodney had another idea. He made an invention to help Ms. Green pass back homework. Rodney opened a latch on the box. "You put the homework in here," he said as he showed Ms. Green the box. "And the homework comes out here."

Rodney pressed a button and a sheet of homework shot across the room. Then all the other papers went flying up into the air. It took a long time to clean them up! Ms. Green was not happy. "A good inventor never gives up," Rodney said.

One day, Rodney said, "I've made the best invention of my life." The class groaned.

"What does it do?" asked Ms. Green, trying to smile.

"It will clean our room," Rodney said. He showed the class his invention. It was a tall box. "Watch," said Rodney. He reached into the box and the box began to shake. Someone yelled, but Rodney smiled. Soon the shaking stopped. Rodney moved the box and under it was a broom!

"Do you like my invention?" Rodney asked.

"We like this new invention," Ms. Green said, and everybody laughed.

"A good inventor never gives up," Rodney said.

Rodney, the Inventor   **35**

Rodney, the Inventor Who Never Gave Up (continued)

Comprehension Activities

Write the answers to the questions on the lines.

1 Why does Rodney say he keeps making new inventions?

_____

_____

2 What is Rodney's problem in this story?

_____

_____

_____

3 How are Rodney's backpack invention and homework invention alike?

_____

_____

_____

Rodney, the Inventor Who Never Gave Up (continued)

4 What would you like to invent? What will it do?

_____

_____

_____

_____

_____

Draw a picture of your invention.

Rodney, the Inventor **37**

| desert | pouch |

The Red Kangaroo

Many different kinds of animals live in the hot, dry desert. Small animals find shade from the hot sun by hiding under the ground. Birds can fly away when it is too hot, but how do the big animals live? Red kangaroos have found many ways to "beat the heat."

Like other big desert animals, kangaroos sleep in the hot hours of the day and are awake when the sun goes down. At night, they look for grass and plants to eat. They look for water to drink. Sometimes, there is little to drink in the desert. Red kangaroos can live with no water for a long time if they have green grass to eat. A red kangaroo has a body that can hold water.

Kangaroos are able to go far to look for food and water. Red kangaroos can hop as fast as 30 miles per hour. They can go a long way with each hop. Did you know that kangaroos can hop, but they can't walk? Their back legs must always move together, not one at a time. To go slow, the kangaroos lean on their tails and front feet. Then they swing their back legs across and back.

When a baby kangaroo is born, it is very small. It lives in its mother's pouch. There, it drinks its mother's milk and keeps growing. After just over 30 weeks in the pouch, the baby is ready to come out. It begins to look around. Soon it will hop through the desert on its own legs.

Comprehension Activities

Write the answers to the questions on the lines.

1 What are two ways red kangaroos "beat the heat" in the desert?

_____

_____

_____

2 It is easy for a kangaroo to go fast but hard for it to go slow. Why is this?

_____

_____

_____

The Red Kangaroo (continued)

3 Where do baby kangaroos live until they are big enough to hop around?

_____

_____

Think of a different animal. Then write the answer to the question on the lines.

4 What kind of animal did you think of?

_____

_____

5 What are two ways your animal and the kangaroo are the *same*?

_____

_____

_____

6 What are two ways your animal and the kangaroo are *different*?

_____

_____

_____

The Red Kangaroo   **39**

| Dr. Art Kramer | professor | psychology | researcher |

Fit Body, Fit Mind

Most of us know that exercise can help keep our bodies fit. Do you know that exercise is good for our minds, too? Exercising can help us think clearly. It can also help us feel happy.

Dr. Art Kramer is a professor of psychology. He teaches about the brain and how it works. He is a researcher, too. He seeks answers to questions. He wanted to know what exercise can do for people's brains. In his research, he asked some people to exercise a lot. He asked others not to exercise at all. Then he tested the people. The tests would help him know how clearly they could think. Dr. Kramer's tests showed him that those who exercised did better on the tests. Exercise helped people to think more clearly.

Dr. Kramer also found that exercise helps older people. It helps them think more clearly. Parts of the brain can get smaller as people get older. This can make it harder to think clearly. When people exercise, these parts of the brain do not get as small. Older people who exercised did better on the tests.

Did you know that exercise can help us feel happy? Researchers say it can. People who were sad said exercise helped them to feel less sad. It is good to know that being fit can help you smile!

What does all of this mean? It means that we should exercise for a fit body and a fit mind. We should walk, run, or swim to help both our body and our mind!

Comprehension Activity

Write your answers to the questions on the lines.

1 What are three ways exercise can help you?

_____

_____

_____

2 How can exercise help older people?

_____

_____

_____

Fit Body, Fit Mind (continued)

3 How does Dr. Kramer know that exercise helps people to think more clearly?

_____

_____

_____

_____

4 What form of exercise do you like? How do you feel after you exercise?

_____

_____

_____

Fit Body, Fit Mind   **41**

double	glared	nickname	practice	worried

Lady Baseball

"Third out!" Meg called, holding up the baseball after her diving catch. Meg ran in and the other team glared at her as they passed. Meg was not only the best baseball player on her team, she was also the only girl on the team.

Even the newest player, Tim, gave Meg a sharp look as he popped her a high five. "Not bad for a girl," he said.

"A lady, you mean," said Meg.

"Yeah, Lady Baseball," he snapped.

As she walked home, Meg talked to her best friend Sara. "Those boys are upset because you're so good," she told Meg with a small smile.

"I know," Meg said. "It would be more fun if we all could be friends."

The next day, Sara, who was sick a lot, was not at school again. Meg began to worry because Sara seemed so tired all the time. Meg hoped that there wasn't anything wrong.

At baseball practice, Meg dropped an easy fly ball, struck out, and later fell while running to first base. Tim helped her up.

"What's wrong?" he asked.

Meg kicked the dirt and said, "Sara's sick again."

The next time Meg was at bat, Tim yelled, "Go, Lady Baseball!" Meg couldn't help but smile at that, and when other players yelled it too, Meg hit a double. It made her feel good to hear them cheer.

The next day, just before the baseball game, Tim asked Meg about Sara. "I talked with her last night," Meg said, "and she will soon be back at school. The doctor says she is going to be fine."

"I'm glad," said Tim. "Let's play ball."

Meg started to think about baseball and everyone cheered when Lady Baseball made a diving catch to win the game.

Lady Baseball (continued)

Comprehension Activity

Write the answers to the questions on the lines.

1 At the beginning of the story, why are the boys upset with Meg?

_____

_____

2 Why does Meg play badly at baseball practice?

_____

_____

3 Tim calls Meg "Lady Baseball." How does he use the nickname the first time he says it? How does he use the nickname later?

_____

_____

_____

Lady Baseball **43**

buzzed	classmates	joked	weekend

A New Start

Linda woke up before her clock buzzed. She was upset. It was her first day at a new school, and she did not know what it would be like.

Linda's family had just moved to a new town. Linda was upset about leaving her school, friends, and home behind. Her mom got a new job, so the family moved right away. Linda was unhappy about not ending third grade with her friends.

While her dad drove Linda to school, she talked about all of the questions she had. How would she find her classroom? Would she make new friends?

When she got to the school, a teacher walked Linda to Mrs. Smith's classroom. "This is Mrs. Smith's classroom. I'm glad you're here," said Mrs. Smith.

"Thank you," Linda said.

Just then, the bell rang and Linda's new classmates began coming in. Linda felt upset again. Would her classmates like her? Would she be eating lunch alone?

It turned out that Linda's desk was right next to Tina's. Tina came over to Linda right away and told Linda the names of all the kids in the class.

At lunch time, Linda felt too shy to ask Tina to eat with her. Before Linda could worry much about it, Tina saw Linda. She asked Linda to have lunch with her. While they ate, Linda and Tina talked and joked like they had been friends for ages!

At the end of the day, Tina asked Linda to come to her house. She was hoping that Linda's mom and dad would let her come over that weekend.

When Linda met her dad outside, he asked, "How was your first day?"

Linda smiled and said, "It was fun, Dad! I made a new friend! I don't know what I was so scared about!"

A New Start (continued)

Comprehension Activity

Circle the letter of the best answer for each question.

1 Why was Linda feeling scared?
   a. She woke up too early for school.
   b. It was the last day of school.
   c. It was the first day at a new school.

2 What happened when Linda walked into the lunchroom?
   a. Tina asked Linda to have lunch with her.
   b. Linda found a spot to sit down alone.
   c. Tina laughed at Linda.

3 From what you read, how do you think Linda felt at the end of the day?
   a. sad
   b. happy
   c. scared

A New Start   **45**

area	field	recycling	sign	Yama

Making a Difference

Bill, Yama, and Jack were best friends. The three boys did everything together. On the way home from school one day, they were talking about their field trip and recycling. They saw how easy it was to recycle things like cans, paper, and glass.

Yama said, "It's too bad we don't have a way to recycle around here. We would have less litter on the streets."

Jack added, "It would make the area cleaner."

Bill snapped his fingers and said, "I've got it! We can start a recycling group! I'll bet my dad will let us pick up cans and paper in front of his store!"

The boys talked to Bill's father about their plan, and he said it was a good idea. With the help of their families, the boys used wood and nails given by a store owner to make a recycling bin.

Bill's father let the boys make a sign about the new recycling bin for his store window. A few people began dropping off paper and cans in the bin. Bill, Yama, and Jack asked the other store owners if they could make signs for their stores, too. They all said yes.

The boys sorted the recycling bin every few days, and Bill's father would drive them to the recycling site to drop off the cans and paper.

People liked to recycle. They saw that since people started recycling, there was not as much litter on the sidewalks. The boys took the money they got from recycling and planted flowers in big pots outside of each store on the block. Their hard work made it a nicer area for everyone to live.

Making a Difference (continued)

Comprehension Activity

Circle the letter of the best answer for each question.

1 Why did the boys want to start recycling?

    a. to clean up the area

    b. to make money

    c. it was their homework

2 What happened just after the boys made the recycling bin?

    a. They planted flowers.

    b. They talked about the field trip.

    c. They made a sign.

3 What was the outcome of recycling in the story?

    a. The area was cleaner.

    b. The boys had fun.

    c. The boys worked together.

Learn About Words

Underline the nouns and circle the verb.

1 Bill talked to his father.

2 People filled the recycling bin.

3 Everyone likes the new flowers.

Making a Difference   **47**

| America | Appaloosa | Native American | Morgan | soldiers |

Horses of America

Explorers came to America in the 1500s. They brought horses with them. They explored America on horseback. Some horses got away. Many free horses were born.

Native Americans found a use for these horses. They rode them to hunt for food. They used horses to carry goods. They used horses to move their homes from place to place. Native Americans took good care of their horses.

People in America found horses to be helpful. They trained horses to pull carts. They trained them to help with the farming. Ranchers rode horses to move herds of cows. Horses were used to help build railroads. Soldiers moved around on horseback. Horses helped with many jobs in America.

Today, horses still work. Officers in cities ride horses. People ride horses where cars cannot go. Ranchers use horses for herding. People also ride horses for fun and exercise.

You can find horses in sport, too. One sport is horse racing. Some horses run short races. Others run long races. In some races, the horses jump over fences. People also show horses. The best-looking horse wins first prize.

Caring for horses is a big job. They need exercise every day. They need good food to eat. Horses must be brushed. Their stalls must be kept clean.

There are many kinds of horses. There are Morgans, Appaloosas, and others. The Morgan is good for riding and pulling carts. The Appaloosa is a strong horse for doing work. In the West, wild horses still run free.

Horses of America (continued)

Comprehension Activities

Circle the letter of the best answer for each question.

1 Which job is one that a horse might do?

    a. help pick crops by hand

    b. help move heavy things

    c. help write a story

2 Which three things do horses need?

    a. exercise, good food, clean stalls

    b. a race, a cart, horseshoes

    c. a job, exercise, a place to run free

3 How did horses help Native Americans?

    a. Horses helped them pull carts.

    b. Horses helped them hunt.

    c. Horses helped them build railroads.

Learn About Words

In the sentences below, circle the adjectives that go with the underlined nouns.

1 The horse pulled the heavy <u>cart</u>.

2 I saw a tall <u>horse</u>.

3 That horse has black <u>hair</u>.

Horses of America   **49**

| apartment | blanket | clues | Strawberry | wrote |

The Case of the Missing Bear

Chad was three years old. He had a soft red teddy bear named Strawberry. Strawberry was his best buddy, and Chad couldn't sleep without him.

One day after lunch, Chad couldn't find Strawberry. He looked all over his room. He asked his brother Mike if he had seen Strawberry.

"No, I haven't seen Strawberry today," said Mike. Chad got upset.

"I can't find him!" he sobbed.

"Let me help you," said Mike. "We can crack the case of the missing teddy bear!"

Mike got a pen and paper to write down clues. He asked, "Where did you last see Strawberry?"

Chad answered, "He was on my bed this morning."

"Who could have moved Strawberry?" asked Mike.

"Mom could have washed him. He was a little dirty," said Chad. "Dad could have put him in the kitchen. Strawberry likes to help Dad make dinner."

Mike wrote down the clues. First, they asked their mom if she took Strawberry to wash him.

She said that she hadn't seen Strawberry all day. Then they asked their dad if he had Strawberry. He said he didn't know where Strawberry was.

Mike took his mom and dad off his list. Then he had a super idea! Mike said they could go to all the spots that Chad went that day to try to find the bear.

First, the boys checked Chad's bed. They took off all the blankets, but there was no Strawberry. Next, they went to the kitchen. They peeked under chairs and tables, but no Strawberry. They looked around the apartment, but did not find Strawberry.

Just when Chad was afraid he had lost Strawberry for good, he remembered that he went to his friend's apartment to play after lunch. Chad and Mike ran out into the hallway. There on the floor was Strawberry!

Chad picked his bear up and gave him a squeeze! Chad thanked Mike for helping him find Strawberry. Chad and Mike took Strawberry to Chad's room and tucked him into bed.

50 *The Case of the Missing Bear*

The Case of the Missing Bear (continued)

Comprehension Activity

Circle A, B, or C.

1 What was Chad missing?
  a. his stuffed dog
  b. his teddy bear
  c. his blanket

2 Why do you think Mike wrote down the clues?
  a. so he could remember them all
  b. so he could write a story about them
  c. so he could tell his mom and dad about them

3 Where was Strawberry found?
  a. in the kitchen
  b. in Chad's bed
  c. in the hallway

Learn About Words

Circle the verb in each sentence.

1 The teddy bear fell on the floor.

2 Chad cried about Strawberry.

3 Mike and Chad cheered.

4 Mike wrote down the clues.

5 They looked around the apartment

The Case of the Missing Bear **51**

Name _____ Date _____

Antarctica

Pack your warmest clothes! You're going on a trip. You are going to Antarctica! "Where is that?" you ask. Antarctica is the continent that is the farthest south. It's a long plane ride away. It will take many hours to go that far south. Your plane may have to make a few stops along the way.

You have heard of the North Pole. You know it is very cold there. Do you know where the South Pole is? The South Pole is in Antarctica. It is very cold there, too. It is almost covered with ice. Most of the ice found in the world is in and around Antarctica. It is the coldest and windiest place on

They go to learn about the land, plants, and animals. These scientists stay indoors most of the time.

There is land under the ice of Antarctica. Not much is known about the land. Scientists do know that there are mountains under the ice. Some of the mountains were made by ice rubbing against rock. Not many plants can live in Antarctica. In some places, you won't find any plants at all. You could not have a garden in Antarctica!

You won't find many animals there. One animal you will find is a penguin. Penguins can

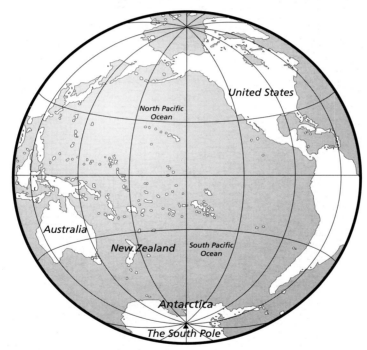

Earth! Winters are very cold. The winter sun does not rise for about six months. This makes winter very dark all day. The sun shines almost all day in the summer. It is still cold in the summer. It never gets warm enough to melt much of the ice.

Not many people live in Antarctica. Even fewer people stay during the winter months. Scientists from all over the world go to Antarctica.

live in Antarctica because they like the cold. Also, they are not bothered much by other animals. Penguins have a layer of fat. It helps to keep them warm. They can keep warm in very cold water. Other animals live around Antarctica. Seals, fish, and dolphins are able to live in the cold water around this very cold continent.

Antarctica (continued)

Comprehension Activities

Circle the letter of the best answer for each question.

1 Which sentence would be the best topic sentence for this passage, the sentence that tells what the passage is about?

   a. Antarctica is a cold place.
   b. Antarctica is not an easy place to live.
   c. Penguins live in Antarctica.

2 Why doesn't the ice on Antarctica melt in the summer?

   a. It is too windy.
   b. The sun doesn't rise.
   c. It never gets warm enough.

3 What helps penguins stay warm in cold areas?

   a. their wings
   b. a layer of fat
   c. a nest

Learn About Words

For each word below, circle the letter for the word with the opposite meaning.

1 cold

   a. chilly
   b. hot
   c. cool

2 south

   a. east
   b. west
   c. north

3 under

   a. below
   b. over
   c. away

Antarctica   **53**

favorite	Jessica	picnic	promised

Sledding with Grandpa

It was a Saturday morning. Jessica was up, dressed, and ready to go. She was waiting for her grandfather's car to pull up. It had snowed during the night, and a beautiful white blanket of snow covered the ground.

Once a month, Jessica's grandfather would take her out for the day. Jessica looked forward to their special Saturdays together. They would talk on the phone to plan their time together. They always chose to do something fun. One day last summer, they took a picnic to the beach and went swimming. Last fall they picked apples. On this winter day, they were going sledding.

Grandpa pulled into the driveway. Jessica helped him strap the sled on top of his car. They both hopped into the car like excited children.

Grandpa and Jessica drove to the sledding hill where he used to take Jessica's father when he was young. Grandpa said some of his happiest moments were on this sledding hill. Grandpa pulled the sled up to the top of the hill. Jessica was afraid of going down the hill too fast, so Grandpa got on the sled behind her. He promised that he would slow the sled down if it went too fast.

Down the hill they went! Jessica was not afraid at all. She laughed when the snow sprayed in her face at the bottom of the hill. Grandpa laughed too.

Grandpa and Jessica slid down the hill again and again. They slid down a different way each time. Sometimes Jessica rode in front of Grandpa. Sometimes she rode behind Grandpa. Once they tried to go backwards. Another time, they tried to go sideways. That time they landed face-first in the snow! Their faces were wet, but they were laughing!

After that, Jessica and Grandpa went to Grandpa's house to warm up. Grandpa made lunch. He made Jessica's favorite soup. While they ate, Grandpa told stories about sledding many years ago. He and Jessica's dad used to slide down the same hill. Jessica said that when she grows up, she will tell her own stories about sledding with Grandpa.

Sledding with Grandpa (continued)

Comprehension Activity

Circle the letter of the best answer for each question.

1 How often did Jessica have a special day with Grandpa?

  a. once a week
  b. once a month
  c. once a year

2 Why did Grandpa pick that sledding hill?

  a. It was the hill where he took Jessica's dad.
  b. It was the nearest hill.
  c. It was the best hill for sledding.

3 What happened when Grandpa and Jessica went down the hill sideways?

  a. They made it all the way to the bottom of the hill.
  b. They landed face-first in the snow.
  c. They met Jessica's dad at the bottom of the hill.

Learn About Words

One good way to learn words is to use them. Look at the number at the end of each sentence. Find the paragraph in the story with the same number. Then find the best word to fill the blank. Write the word.

1 _____ is a winter activity you can do in the snow. (2)

2 Grandpa had many happy _____ sledding with Jessica's father. (4)

3 Jessica laughed as snow _____ in her face the first time she went down the

hill. (5)

Sledding with Grandpa **55**

| aunt | fields | invited | surprise |

Carl's Summer on the Farm

It was the last day of school, and Carl was looking forward to spending his summer playing with his friends. They had planned a lot of fun things to do. That night, Carl's mom said, "I have a surprise for you. Your Uncle Bill and Aunt Fern have invited you to spend the summer with them on their farm."

The next day, Carl's mom drove him to the farm. Carl missed his friends already. His mom kept telling him that he would have a great time on the farm, but Carl was not so sure.

The first night on the farm, Carl realized how quiet it was. He didn't hear any of the usual city noise. It was so quiet that it was hard for Carl to sleep. In the morning, Uncle Bill woke Carl up very early, saying, "It's time to milk the cows." Carl couldn't believe that he had to do chores.

That first day on the farm was very hard. First Carl helped Uncle Bill take care of the animals, and then he helped Aunt Fern weed the garden. After supper, they sat outside and ate Aunt Fern's ice cream. They talked a bit and listened to the soft sounds of evening.

Carl quickly got used to life on the farm. After the chores were done, there was time for fun. Some days they would go swimming in the river, or Carl would take long bike rides along the dirt roads. On other days, Carl and his aunt would go bird-watching. Carl even began to like doing his chores! He talked to the animals while he fed them, and he and his uncle told silly jokes as they worked in the fields. Carl never laughed so hard in his life.

The summer went by very quickly. When he got back to the city, Carl was surprised at how noisy it was. He missed his aunt and uncle and all of the animals on the farm. It felt good to be home, but Carl hoped that he could spend next summer on the farm again.

Comprehension Activity

Circle the letter of the best answer for each question.

1 Which word best tells how Carl first felt about the idea of going to a farm?
 a. unhappy
 b. pleased
 c. afraid

2 What did Carl learn in this story?
 a. You can't have fun without your friends.
 b. The city is the best place to live.
 c. It can be fun to try new things.

3 When Carl returned home at the end of the summer, why did he think the city was noisy?
 a. He was used to the quiet at the farm.
 b. The city had changed while he was away.
 c. His friends said it was too noisy.

Carl's Summer on the Farm (continued)

Learn About Words

For each word below, circle the letter for the word with the opposite meaning.

1 awake

 a. up
 b. happy
 c. asleep

2 friendly

 a. nice
 b. mean
 c. kind

3 stand

 a. step
 b. walk
 c. sit

Thomas Edison	lightbulb	machine	phonograph	record

Thomas Edison

Thomas Edison lived from 1847 until 1931. As a child, he did not go to school for very long. Instead, his mother and father were his teachers. He liked to read and find out about things. He liked to try new ideas. He would invent things to help make people's lives better or more fun.

Somebody else had made a new tool called a telephone. Edison's ears did not work very well. It was hard for him to hear a voice on the telephone. He found a way to make the sound louder. The tool Edison made is still used in telephones today. Without Thomas Edison, you might not be able to hear the other person when you answer the telephone.

Of all the new tools Edison made, one of the most important is the phonograph. Edison's phonograph was the first tool that could record a sound and play it back. The first phonograph worked with the help of some tinfoil. When you hear a CD or listen to voice mail, you can thank Thomas Edison!

Thomas Edison did not make the first lightbulb. He did make the first lightbulb that would stay lit for many hours! It was the first lightbulb that could light homes for many hours.

How would power for the lightbulbs get to the homes? Edison had the answer. He found a way to bring power to many homes all at once. Without Edison's ideas, you might still need a fire to see at night!

Have you watched a movie lately? Thank Thomas Edison! He was one of the first makers of moving pictures. Now we call them "movies." He made a machine to take the movies. He made another machine to show the movies.

Thomas Edison was always looking for new ways of doing things. His ideas have made our lives better and more fun.

Comprehension Activity

Circle the letter of the best answer for each question.

1 What is this story about?

  a. when Thomas Edison was a child
  b. Thomas Edison's mother and father
  c. things that Thomas Edison invented

2 How was Edison's telephone better than the first telephones?

  a. It was louder.
  b. It was easy to use.
  c. It did not need a wire.

3 What could happen because of Thomas Edison's lightbulb?

  a. People could see at night.
  b. Light could be used outside.
  c. Lights could stay lit a long time.

Thomas Edison (continued)

Learn About Words

Look at these word parts and what they mean:

graph – writing, recording	*micro* – small	*phone, phono* – sound	*tele* – far, distant

Now look at these words. Use the word parts to figure out what they mean.

microphone   phonograph   telegraph   telephone

Write each word by its meaning.

1 machine that records sound _____

2 machine that writes far away _____

3 machine that takes sound far away _____

4 machine that takes a small sound and makes it bigger _____

Thomas Edison   **59**

Name _____ Date _____

| Mercury | Venus | Mars | Jupiter | Saturn | Uranus |
| Neptune | | Pluto | | dwarf | |

The Planets in Our Solar System

Earth is just one of eight planets in a huge group. All of the planets move around the sun. Mercury, Venus, Earth, and Mars are all rocky planets. Jupiter, Saturn, Uranus, and Neptune are made mostly of gases.

Mercury is closest to the sun, so it can get hotter there than any other planet. Because it doesn't have any air to hold heat in, it can get very cold at night.

The next planet is Venus. Venus has thick clouds around it that keep heat inside, so it is hot. Sunlight bounces off the clouds, making Venus visible from Earth.

Earth is the third planet from the sun. Much of Earth is covered by water. Earth has four seasons because of the way it spins as it moves around the sun.

Mars is the next planet. Special robots have landed on Mars and found proof of water there. If there is or once was water on Mars, there could be some living things on Mars that we have not found yet.

Jupiter is the next planet, and it is the largest. It is more like a large, hot star than a planet, and it would be a star if it were much larger. Jupiter has 63 moons, more than any other planet.

Saturn has rings around it. Scientists think these rings are made of water and ice. The winds on Saturn are very fast, making Saturn look like a striped planet.

The next planet is Uranus. It is so far from the sun that it takes 84 years to go around the Sun once. Each season on Uranus is 20 years long.

Neptune is the farthest planet from the sun. You need special tools to see it because it is so far away. It takes 165 years for Neptune to go around the sun.

What about Pluto? Until 2006, Pluto was thought to be the farthest planet from the sun. Scientists decided to change the definition of a planet, so Pluto is now called a dwarf planet. The more scientists study the planets, the more they learn about them.

60   *The Planets in Our Solar System*

60   Leveled Passages

The Planets in Our Solar System (continued)

Comprehension Activity

Circle the letter of the best answer for each question.

1 Which planet is closest to the sun?

  a. Jupiter
  b. Mercury
  c. Earth

2 Which sentence best tells the main idea of this passage?

  a. Neptune is the farthest planet from the sun.
  b. Planets move around the sun.
  c. Eight planets move around our sun.

3 Which sentence best describes Earth?

  a. Earth, like Pluto, is far from the sun.
  b. Earth is a rocky planet covered mostly by water.
  c. Earth is a large planet made up of many gases.

Learn About Words

You can often tell the meaning of a word by reading the words around it. Find the word in the story that matches the definition. The paragraph number in parentheses will help you find the word. Then write the word after its definition.

1 objects in space that move around the sun (1) _____

2 spring, summer, winter, fall (4) _____

3 not a planet, not a moon, but a very large, hot object in space (6) _____

The Planets in Our Solar System **61**

beachcombing	parents	speckled

Beachcombing

A large, gray beach house stands on the white sands of the beach right beside the sea. Outside the open window of the house, the early morning sky slowly grows. The sound of waves crashing softly on the shore is joined by the sharp cry of sea birds. Inside, three children stir in their beds, opening their eyes. Emma, Rose, and Jake dash to the window and sniff the salt air.

"Come on," Rose says. "Let's get Mom and Dad. I want to go out and play on the beach."

"Me too!" shout Emma and Jake. "Wake up, Mom and Dad, and let's go beachcombing!"

While their parents yawn, the three children jump into their clothes and grab their pails for the beach. The front door flies open and bare feet hurry across the smooth boards of the old, worn deck. The whole family runs together, laughing, from the deck across the sand toward the foaming waves. The water feels warm as it washes over their legs and the children run back and forth, chasing the waves for a few minutes. Then Rose comes running to her parents, holding a speckled shell in her small, wet fingers.

"What is this, Mom?" she asks her mother.

"That's a seashell, Rose," says Mom. "Hold it to your ear, and tell me if you can you hear the sound of the sea."

The three children take turns holding the shell to their ears as they listen to the soft whisper that sounds like the roaring of the sea. Rose listens one last time before she puts the shell in her pail.

"Let's go find some more shells!" shouts Emma.

The children dash around the beach, picking up shells of different colors and shapes. They find white shells and yellow ones, brown shells and gold ones. Some shells are large and speckled, while others are tiny and pale. Some shells are covered with sharp little points, while others feel smooth like glass. Soon all three pails are filled with many kinds of shells. The shells spill over the tops until the pails are almost—but not quite—too heavy for the children to carry.

Tired but happy, Emma, Rose, and Jake dance across the hot sand and back to the beach house. They will spend their afternoon sitting on the beach-house deck, sorting and counting their treasures from the sea.

Comprehension Activities

Circle the letter of the best answer for each question.

1 Where is the family in this story taking a vacation?

    a. at the beach

    b. in the desert

    c. in the mountains

2 What are the children in the story doing?

    a. climbing trees

    b. playing volleyball

    c. looking for seashells

Beachcombing (continued)

3 How do Emma, Rose, and Jake feel at the beginning of the story?
   a. afraid
   b. hungry
   c. excited

4 Why do the children hold the shell to their ears?
   a. to feel how heavy it is
   b. to hear the sound it makes
   c. to empty the sand out of it

Write the answers to the questions on the lines.

5 What are three sounds that people hear in the story?

_____

_____

_____

6 What does "treasures from the sea" mean at the very end of the story?

_____

_____

_____

7 What are three different ways the children could sort their shells?

_____

_____

_____

Beachcombing   **63**

Name _____ Date _____

| fir | forester | logger | moss |

At Work in the Forest

Hi! I'm a forester. My name is Jenny, and my job is to take care of the forest. The forest is an important and wonderful place. Come along with me and I will show you why! It's a very nice morning as we set out to learn about the forest. The bright smell of pine and fir greets our noses,

and a blazing, blue sky lights the tops of the trees. Along the path are patches of soft, green moss. Flowers line the trail, adding their own sweet smell to the summer air. Birds sing above us, and a squirrel barks at us from the top of a tall tree.

Soon, another sound reaches our ears. Shouts and laughter float on the breeze and a motor hums to life. Men are at work in the forest with big saws! These men are called loggers. They cut down trees, nip off the branches, and load the logs into trucks. The trucks carry the logs down the mountain to the mill, where the logs will be cut into boards. My job is to help the loggers decide which trees to cut down.

We leave the loggers and go a little farther on the mountain road, where we come to another group of people working. Instead of cutting down trees, these people plant new trees! This part of the forest was burned in a fire a few years ago, and the workers are planting trees to take the place of those that burned. These people also plant trees in areas where the trees have been cut down by loggers. To plant a tree, the worker swings a heavy tool, making a hole in the hard soil. Working fast, he pulls a tiny baby tree from the heavy bag on his belt and sticks it quickly into the hole. The worker will plant many hundreds of trees today. Before long, a new forest will grow from the ashes of the old.

Our forests give us wood to build our homes, schools, and stores. They give us good places to camp, walk, and fish. I am proud of the important work I do, helping to take care of our forests. Maybe someday you will want to go to work in the forest, too!

At Work in the Forest (continued)

Comprehension Activity

Circle the letter of the best answer for each question.

1 The person who is telling this story works

   a. on a ship.

   b. in a forest.

   c. in an office.

2 At the mill in the story, the trees are cut into

   a. paper.

   b. boards.

   c. branches.

3 Part of the forest is in ashes because of

   a. a fire.

   b. a strong wind.

   c. road construction.

Learn About Words

Many job names end with *-er*. Write the name of the person that does each job.

1 Cuts down trees for logs _____

2 Plants new trees _____

3 Takes care of the forest _____

At Work in the Forest **65**

bravery	caught	chewed	climbed	lion

The Lion and the Mouse

One day, a lion was sleeping in the tall grass, when a tiny mouse decided to have some fun. The mouse began running all over the lion's back!

The lion felt a tickle on his back and sat up suddenly. The mouse froze, hoping the lion wouldn't spot him. The lion turned his head and was shocked to see a mouse standing on his back.

The mouse tried to run away, but when he did, the lion placed his big paw on the mouse's tail. Although the mouse was small, the lion was really hungry. He leaned over to eat the mouse.

When he realized that he was about to be eaten, the mouse said, "Wait, great lion." The lion was stunned to meet a mouse who was so brave to talk to him.

The lion asked, "What do you want?"

The mouse cried, "Please, lion, if you let me go, I will never forget it."

The lion laughed. "Why should I let you go? Why should I care about what you think?"

"If you let me go, maybe I will be able to do something nice for you in return someday," said the mouse.

The lion laughed so loudly that the ground shook. "What can a tiny mouse do for a great lion?" But he was stunned by the mouse's bravery, so he let the mouse go.

A few days later, the lion was caught in a hunter's trap. The hunter wanted to take the lion to the king as a gift, so he went to get his wagon. The hunter left the lion tied to a tree.

The lion was not able to get away. While he sat there feeling sorry for himself, the tiny mouse happened to walk by. "What happened to you?" asked the mouse.

"I got caught in a hunter's trap. Now he's going to take me to the king, and who knows what will happen to me there," said the lion sadly.

The mouse remembered how the lion had let him go. He wasn't going to forget how kind the lion had been to him. So the mouse climbed up on the lion's back. He chewed on the rope that kept the lion tied to the tree. Finally, he chewed all the way through and freed the lion. The lion was thankful that the mouse saved his life, and they became friends forever.

The Lion and the Mouse (continued)

Comprehension Activity

Circle the letter of the best answer for each question.

1 Which character helps the other first in this story?

    a. the lion

    b. the mouse

    c. the hunter

2 In what way are the mouse and the lion in this story like people?

    a. They chew ropes.

    b. They roar.

    c. They talk.

3 Which sentence best tells the lesson learned in this story?

    a. Little friends can be good friends.

    b. Always trust a mouse.

    c. Lions always get away.

Learn About Words

Read each sentence from the story. Then choose the two words that combine to make the underlined contraction in the sentence.

1 Now <u>he's</u> going to take me to the king.

    a. he sees

    b. he was

    c. he is

2 He <u>wasn't</u> going to forget how kind the lion had been to him.

    a. was not

    b. were not

    c. will not

3 The mouse froze, hoping the lion <u>wouldn't</u> spot him.

    a. was not

    b. would not

    c. would have

The Lion and the Mouse **67**

| awards | concert | donated | musicians | Roberta Guaspari | violin |

The Music of Life

Roberta Guaspari is a music teacher in New York City. She teaches the violin to children. She teaches in the part of the city called Harlem. Harlem is a poorer part of New York City. When she started teaching in the 1980s, there was not much music in the schools.

Ms. Guaspari loved the children. She loved teaching music. The children loved learning music. They loved learning to play the violin. But in 1991, New York City schools had no money for the music program. Ms. Guaspari was afraid she would no longer have a job.

She wanted to save the music program. She wanted to keep the music alive in the schools. She wrote letters to everyone she thought could help. Then a story about her students was in the New York Times newspaper. She also told her story on TV.

People were interested in her work. Her violin students performed in a concert. They called the concert of violins Fiddlefest. Well-known musicians came to the concert. They wanted to hear the students play. They liked what they heard. The musicians donated their time and money so the students could have music lessons. They asked others to give money.

They raised enough money to keep the school music program going. Ms. Guaspari also opened a music center. At the center, students learn to play the violin even if they cannot pay for lessons.

Ms. Guaspari knows music makes a difference for children. Music students do better in school. They make something delightful with their music. This makes them proud. It makes them feel good. The music students have played for Presidents. They have played in movies. They have been on TV. They have traveled far to other countries to play music. They have played with well-known musicians.

Ms. Guaspari wrote a book. It is about her life and her work. The book is called *Music of the Heart*. Her story was made into two movies. The movies are *Small Wonders* and *Music of the Heart*.

Ms. Guaspari has earned many awards for her teaching. She has been praised for bringing music to the children of New York City. Her music program began in just one classroom. Now it brings music to thousands of children.

The Music of Life (continued)

Comprehension Activity

Circle the letter of the best answer for each question.

1 What kind of writing is this selection?
  a. fiction
  b. nonfiction
  c. fantasy

2 From what you read, which word best describes Roberta Guaspari?
  a. quiet
  b. the outdoor-type
  c. firm

3 What happened after Ms. Guaspari was on TV to tell her story?
  a. Her music program ended.
  b. People donated money to keep the music program going.
  c. Other music teachers offered their time to keep the program going.

Learn About Words

Circle A, B, or C to choose the synonym of the underlined word.

1 Musicians <u>donated</u> their time and money.
  a. gave
  b. counted
  c. took

2 The music students have <u>played</u> for Presidents.
  a. voted
  b. met
  c. performed

3 They make something <u>delightful</u> with their music.
  a. ugly
  b. pleasing
  c. loud

The Music of Life **69**

| apologized | pouted | request | shelter | volunteers |

Gabby Learns a Lesson

Gabby was used to getting things her way all the time. If there was a new toy she wanted, her mother and father got it for her. After school every day, she got to do whatever she wanted. She never had to help around the house, and she never had to do any chores at all. You might say that Gabby was a spoiled, selfish child.

Since Gabby always got her way, you might also think that she was happy with her life. Instead, Gabby was unhappy and she pouted all the time. The more she got, the more she thought she should get. She expected her friends to do what she wanted all the time. She thought her friends should share with her, but she didn't share with them. One by one, her friends stopped spending time with her. Gabby couldn't understand why her friends didn't want to be around her anymore. She didn't see that the way she treated her friends drove them away.

One Saturday, Gabby was pouting because she had no friends to play with her. Her mom was getting ready to go help at a shelter for homeless people. She helped serve lunch almost every Saturday. Since Gabby had nothing else to do, she asked her mom if she could go too. Gabby's mom was stunned by Gabby's request. She told Gabby that she would be expected to help serve lunch,

and no one would be serving her. Gabby's mom was even more shocked when Gabby said, "Okay. Let's go."

When they got to the shelter, Gabby saw children waiting with their parents for a hot meal. Gabby worked very hard to help her mom and the other volunteers who were serving lunch to the families.

When Gabby took a break, she watched the families eating together. They talked and laughed while they ate. Although they didn't have a lot of things, they seemed happy. It made Gabby feel good to think that she helped bring smiles to their faces. It was then that Gabby realized that this good feeling was something new for her.

When Gabby got home, she thought for a long time about how she had been acting. She knew she had not been very nice to her friends. She apologized to her parents for pouting and for not helping them more. She wanted to make a change. From then on, Gabby helped her mom at the shelter every Saturday. She smiled instead of pouted and she was kind and shared her toys. She won back her old friends, and she made new friends too. Gabby had learned an important lesson.

Gabby Learns a Lesson (continued)

Comprehension Activity

Circle the letter of the best answer for each question.

1 Which word describes Gabby at the beginning of the story?

a. kind

b. spoiled

c. forgetful

2 What happens after Gabby helps at the shelter?

a. She changes the way she acts.

b. She never goes to the shelter again.

c. She goes home and plays with her toys.

3 What lesson does Gabby learn in this story?

a. It's nice to get your own way.

b. Help yourself, not others.

c. Helping others makes you feel good.

Learn About Words

Read each sentence. Then circle the letter for the word in the sentence that contains a suffix.

1 At the end of the story, Gabby is a helpful child.

a. helpful

b. story

c. end

2 Gabby's mom kindly helps out at the shelter.

a. shelter

b. out

c. kindly

3 Someone who doesn't share might be a selfish person.

a. selfish

b. doesn't

c. someone

Gabby Learns a Lesson **71**

| camera | computer | cousin | museum | photography |

A Family Story

Eddie was interested in photography. He loved to read books about it. He liked looking at old family photos. He often went to the photography shows at the museum. On Eddie's birthday, he got the gift he really wanted. He got a camera.

Eddie wanted his photos to be interesting and fun. He wanted his photos to tell a story. Eddie looked around him. He saw new leaves on the trees. He saw spring flowers on the bushes. It was all very pretty, but it was not what Eddie wanted to show in his photos.

Eddie's mom and dad were planting flowers in the garden. Eddie's sister, Amanda, was riding her bike around and around. This was neither fun nor interesting. This was everyday stuff.

Then Eddie heard Mom laugh. She had slipped in the garden. She was sitting in the dirt. Eddie snapped a picture! As Dad helped Mom stand up, Dad slipped too. Now they were both sitting in the dirt. They were both laughing. Eddie snapped another picture.

Suddenly Amanda rode up close to Eddie. She yelled, "Take a picture of me! Try to catch me!" Eddie pushed the button as Amanda zoomed away.

Eddie took more pictures that day. He took a photo of his aunt and uncle as they drove up in their car. He took a photo of his cousins getting out of the car. He took a photo of his oldest cousin holding his new baby cousin. Eddie even took a picture of himself. He held his arms out as far as he could. He aimed the camera at his face. Snap!

That evening, Eddie linked the camera up to the computer. This way he could see the photos on the screen. Eddie smiled. Here were the things that had happened that day. Amanda's hair was flying out as she rode her bike. Mom and Dad were laughing like kids in the garden. His aunt and uncle were waving from the car window. His cousins were hopping around the car. Eddie was smiling straight into the camera.

Eddie's photos told a story about his family. He printed the photos on the printer. He made a book of blank pages. On each page he put a photo. Then he wrote about each photo. Eddie gave the book to his grandmother.

Eddie and his grandmother sat together to read Eddie's story about their family. Grandmother smiled. She said this was the best story she had ever read.

A Family Story (continued)

Comprehension Activity

Circle A, B, or C.

1 Which sentence best tells the main idea of this selection?

   a. It's fun to take pictures.
   b. Pictures can tell a story.
   c. Eddie is a nice son.

2 At the end of the story, what does Eddie understand about his photos?

   a. He understands that taking photos is not interesting.
   b. He understands that his photos are pretty.
   c. He understands that his photos could tell a story.

3 Which sentence tells you that Eddie's grandmother liked what Eddie did?

   a. Eddie gave the book to his grandmother.
   b. Eddie and his grandmother sat together.
   c. Grandmother said this was the best story she had ever read.

Learn About Words

Circle A, B, or C to choose the part of speech of the underlined word.

1 <u>Mom</u> does not like having her picture taken.

   a. verb
   b. noun
   c. adjective

2 Eddie <u>took</u> a picture of himself.

   a. verb
   b. noun
   c. adjective

3 He took a photo of his <u>oldest</u> cousin.

   a. verb
   b. noun
   c. adjective

A Family Story **73**

| dolphins | guides | healthier | muscles | seizure |

Animal Helpers

You might have heard about dogs that work as guides for people who are blind. You might know about dogs that help people who are in wheelchairs. Do you know that there are other ways that dogs can help people? Do you know that there are other helpful animals, too? Would you be shocked to know that monkeys, horses, and dolphins can help people, too?

Some dogs have an important talent. They can sense when a person is going to have a seizure. No one knows what gives some dogs this unusual talent. Some people who have seizures have found that their dog knows that they are about to be ill. The dog barks or gives a warning to let the person know that they should sit or lie down. The dog then stays with the person until the seizure is over.

Some monkeys can be trained to help people, too. Because monkeys have hands like people do, they can do many things that dogs cannot do. They can pick up things, turn the pages of a book or turn on a light. They help people who cannot do these things for themselves. Monkeys, like other animals, often enjoy being with people. A person with a helpful monkey usually thinks of the monkey as a good friend.

Animals can also help people be healthier. A horse is one such animal. A horse can help people make their muscles stronger. When you walk, you use muscles in your legs and in your sides. These muscles are the same ones you use when riding a horse. When people ride horses, their side muscles get stronger. Stronger side muscles make walking easier. Children who have trouble walking can enjoy the freedom of movement while riding a horse. As they ride, they also make their muscles stronger.

The dolphin is another animal that can help people feel better. Dolphins are very smart animals. They can be trained to let people swim with them. Children and adults who swim with dolphins often feel better about themselves. Most people who swim with dolphins say that it makes them feel happy. Some people are able to do more than they thought they could when they swim with dolphins.

If you have a pet, you know how happy your pet can make you. Now you know that animals not only help make us happy. They can also help us do more and be healthier.

Animal Helpers (continued)

Comprehension Activity

Circle the letter of the best answer for each question.

1 Which sentence best tells the main idea of this selection?

    a. Many animals can help people.
    b. Most people love their pets.
    c. Some people have helpful monkeys.

2 How does riding a horse help people?

    a. Riding helps people like horses.
    b. Riding makes muscles stronger.
    c. Horses make good pets.

3 Based on the information in the selection, which statement is true?

    a. Dolphins make people feel sad.
    b. Monkeys are smart animals.
    c. Horses are smarter than dogs.

Learn About Words

Circle A, B, or C.

1 Which set of words is in alphabetical order?

    a. people, friend, sit
    b. sit, friend, people
    c. friend, people, sit

2 Which word goes between *dog* and *walk* so that the three words are in alphabetical order?

    dog, _____, walk

    a. animal
    b. legs
    c. you

3 Which set of words is NOT in alphabetical order?

    a. work, swim, bark
    b. book, healthy, smart
    c. dolphin, happy, pet

Animal Helpers   **75**

| control | glider | lever | scientists | Orville and Wilbur Wright |

A History of Flight

Have you ever been flying in an airplane? Today air travel is a fast way to get people and things to faraway places. Air travel even took men to the moon. But people did not always fly. In fact, airplanes have been around for just over 100 years.

People first took to the skies in hot-air balloons. The heated air in the big balloon made the balloon go up in the air. People rode in a basket that hung under the balloon. It was hard to control how the hot-air balloon moved. Riders had to travel where the wind took them.

The next air travel invention was the glider. Gliders had to take off from a high place. Again, the gliders could only go where the wind and air took them. The first gliders could not hold a lot of weight. They could not go far. They could not fly on a calm day. Many people worked to make the glider better.

At the end of the 1800s, two brothers named Orville and Wilbur Wright tried to build an airplane. It was powered by an engine, not powered by the wind. The first flight of their airplane was December 17, 1903. In this first airplane flight, the pilot rode on the lower wing. He controlled the airplane with his hips and a hand lever.

Within ten years, pilots were flying airplanes in races. They would fly from one city to another. Everyone wanted airplanes that could fly higher, farther, and faster. Airplane companies around the world began to build airplanes.

Airplanes were first used in battle during World War I. This was around 1914. Today, airplanes fly higher, farther, and faster than those first airplanes. Even the spacecraft of today are based on the ideas of the first airplanes. As you know, spacecraft fly the highest, farthest, and fastest of all.

People are still making airplanes better. Scientists are working on airplanes that fix themselves if something breaks during a flight. Some airplanes are getting better computers. This can help pilots know what is happening around the airplane. They will know what is going on no matter how dark it is or how bad the weather is. Scientists are also trying to make better personal airplanes. This is a plane for just one person. People can fly this airplane without much training. One day you might fly to work or to school. Can you imagine a sky full of airplanes instead of a road full of cars?

A History of Flight (continued)

Comprehension Activity

Circle the letter of the best answer for each question.

1 Which sentence BEST tells the main idea of this selection?

   a. Airplanes have changed a lot.

   b. Airplanes are fun to ride in.

   c. Airplanes were invented over 100 years ago.

2 How has the invention of the airplane changed people's lives?

   a. Everyone flies in personal airplanes.

   b. People can travel farther and faster.

   c. Everyone lives near an airport.

3 How might air travel be different one day?

   a. It might be easy for everyone to fly a plane.

   b. The roads will be filled with airplanes.

   c. People will ride in a basket under a balloon.

Learn About Words

Circle A, B, or C to choose the synonym of the underlined adjective.

1 Today air travel is a <u>fast</u> way to travel.

   a. friendly

   b. slow

   c. quick

2 Gliders could not fly on a <u>calm</u> day.

   a. clean

   b. windless

   c. rough

3 Scientists are also trying to make <u>better</u> personal airplanes.

   a. bad

   b. bitter

   c. greater

A History of Flight   **77**

| Gianni | liberty | Lucia | Napoli, Italy | Paulo |

Going to America in 1898

Paulo and Anna lived in a tiny town in the south of Italy. Their children were Gianni and Lucia. Gianni was ten years old and Lucia was eight years old. They had never lived anywhere else. Paulo was a baker. He did not make much money because the people in town were so poor.

Anna said to Paulo that they might all have a better life in America. They packed two large trunks with everything they owned. Gianni thought it would be a great adventure. Lucia was afraid of being around so many people she did not know.

They took a train to the sea. The children had never been on a train before. At the city of Napoli they met their steamship. Lucia said the ship looked as long as a whole row of houses in their town.

Paulo and his family stayed on a lower deck of the ship. Many of the other people spoke Italian but some did not. Paulo and Gianni slept on bunk beds in a room with the other men. Anna and Lucia stayed with the women. They all ate at long tables. Sometimes people played music and danced. Gianni played games with other boys.

One morning after many long days at sea, Paulo and his family stood on the deck of the ship. The sea was very calm. The sun was rising behind them, and the sky was a clear blue. Birds flew overhead, rising and falling with the wind. All of a sudden they saw Lady Liberty. They had arrived in America.

Two hours later the ship stopped at a large dock. Paulo's family climbed down a ramp behind many other people. A sign read "Ellis Island." A huge crowd of people waited to show papers before passing through an iron gate. To Paulo that crowd seemed as large as the ocean they had just crossed. Paulo and his family waited for their turn.

Finally Paulo and his family rode a much smaller boat from the island. They climbed a set of stone stairs. At the top they discovered a street with lots of very tall buildings. The street was alive with crowds, and there was a lot of noise as people passed Paulo and his family.

"Well, my dears," said Paulo. "We are in our new home. This is America!"

Comprehension Activity

Circle the letter of the best answer for each question.

1 Why did Paulo and Anna move to America?
  a. They had once lived in America.
  b. Gianni and Lucia did not like Italy.
  c. They hoped for a better life.

2 How did Gianni feel about going to America?
  a. He thought it would be an adventure.
  b. He just didn't want to go.
  c. He was afraid.

3 What did Lucia say about the steamship?
  a. It did not look safe.
  b. It looked like the ships docked in their town.
  c. It looked as long as a whole row of houses in their town.

Going to America in 1898 (continued)

4 How did Paulo and his family get to the steamship?

   a. They walked to the steamship.

   b. They took a train to the steamship.

   c. They took a horse and buggy to the steamship.

5 How was the trip to the steamship different for the children?

   a. They had never been on a train before.

   b. The children did not like it.

   c. They slept in different rooms.

6 How did Paulo's family know they had reached America?

   a. They saw an island.

   b. The captain told them.

   c. They saw Lady Liberty.

7 What did the family do right after they got off the ship?

   a. They got into a smaller boat.

   b. They went to Ellis Island.

   c. They took a train ride.

8 To what did Paulo compare the crowd at Ellis Island?

   a. The crowd looked like animals on a farm.

   b. The crowd looked like the ocean they had just crossed.

   c. The crowd looked like the people from their town in Italy.

9 Where was Paulo's family's new home?

   a. America

   b. Napoli

   c. Ellis Island

Going to America in 1898 **79**

Going to America in 1898 (continued)

Learn About Words

Look at each number in parentheses. Find the paragraph in the story with the same number. Then find the word that fits the given meaning. Write your answers on the lines.

1 a fun thing to do (2) _____

2 freedom to think and act without fear (5) _____

3 a sloping walkway (6) _____

4 a piece of land with water all around it (6) _____

5 found (7) _____

80   *Going to America in 1898*

Eric	Jenna	Marcus	Hmm

The Homework Handshake

"Up high, down low, slap me five, way to go," Jeff, Kate, and Eric cheered as they moved their arms and hands up, down, and around in a handshake.

"What are you doing?" Jenna asked. They were in line at the beginning of the school day.

"You always do that handshake," Marcus said.

"Not every day," Eric said. "You'll see. One day you'll get it." Some kids leaned in, hoping Eric would say more. Even their teacher, Mrs. Green, looked at Eric. But Eric didn't say anything else.

As they put their homework in the basket, Jeff, Kate, and Eric smiled. Jenna saw them. "Hmm," she said.

The next day, only Jeff and Eric did the handshake in line. When they turned in their homework, Kate said, "I lost mine."

"Hmm," Jenna said again.

The day after, Jenna slipped into line behind Jeff, Kate, and Eric and said, "I did my homework!" They all did the handshake.

Two days later, Marcus got it. By the end of the week, everybody was doing the handshake, but not Mrs. Green.

For two weeks, they all turned in their homework and did the handshake. Mrs. Green was proud, but she didn't understand. Then one day, Mrs. Green put something in the homework basket. She said, "Can I do the homework handshake, too?"

"You turned in homework, Mrs. Green," Jeff said, "and you got it! You can do the homework handshake, too."

The Homework Handshake (continued)

Comprehension Activity

Write the answers to the questions on the lines.

1 Who are the first three students to do the handshake?

Jeff, Kate, and Eric

2 What does the handshake mean?

Idea: The handshake means that the students turned in their homework.

3 Why is Mrs. Green proud?

Idea: Mrs. Green is proud of the students because they are doing and turning in their homework every day.

4 How do you know that Mrs. Green understands the homework handshake?

Idea: Mrs. Green puts her homework into the basket and then asks to do the handshake.

5 Does this story take place at school or at home? How do you know?

Idea: The story takes place at school. Clues are that the characters are in line before school, and the story mentions a teacher and homework.

---

above	weather

How Is the Weather?

What do you see and feel outside? Is it sunny or raining? Is it hot or cold? Do you know why the weather is different each day?

The air and the ground are heated by the sun. Clouds and gas in the sky trap heat, and that keeps us from getting too cold.

Clouds play a big part in making the weather. Clouds hold in heat at night, make shade by day, and bring us rain and snow. When a cloud holds a lot of water, the water turns into rain. If the air is very cold, the rain may freeze into ice or snow. Can you tell when a cloud is holding a lot of water?

Wind moves weather from one spot to another. Hot air moves up, leaving a space below it, and colder air moves into the space. As hot and cold air move around, they make wind. Wind may blow us hot weather or cold weather.

Wind also moves waves of water from one spot to another. If the water is hot, it heats the air above it and makes the weather hotter. If the water is cold, it cools the air above it and makes the weather colder. When wind moves the waves in the sea, they can bring hot or cold weather to places all around the world.

Waves, sun, wind, and clouds work together to make weather. When you go outside, think about everything that makes the weather what it is!

Comprehension Activities

Write the answers to the questions on the lines.

1 What are three ways clouds make the weather different?

Ideas: Clouds hold in heat during the night. Clouds provide shade during the day. Clouds bring rain and snow.

How Is the Weather? (continued)

2 What are two ways the wind moves weather from one spot to another?

Ideas: The wind blows hot and cold air from one place to another to change the weather. It also moves warmer and cooler water in the sea from one place to another in waves.

Draw pictures to answer the questions. You may have some words in your pictures.

3 How does heat get to the ground and the air? Draw a picture to show your answer.

Pictures will vary, but they should indicate sun heating the ground and the air.

4 What happens when hot air moves up? Draw a picture to show your answer.

Pictures will vary, but they should indicate cold air moving in to replace the hot air that has moved up.

| cancer | doctors | follow | keen | police | scent |

Follow Your Nose, Dog!

If you know dogs, you know they like to follow their noses. They sniff anything from the people they meet to anything on the street. Dogs do this because they have a very good sense of smell. Dogs can smell many times better than people can!

For years, people have used dogs' keen sense of smell to help them. Police use trained dogs to help fight crime and to find things. A dog's nose can track, or follow, the scent of people. They can help the police find people who do not follow the law or people who are missing or trapped.

Dogs can be trained to sniff out some kinds of cancer. These trained dogs use their sense of smell to tell the difference between skin with cancer and skin without cancer. This helps doctors to take care of people so the people can get better. These dogs can help save many lives.

No matter what their job, dogs are trained in much the same way. Often, they find out how to do their job by playing. The trainer throws a rag, and the dog brings it back. Then the trainer adds a smell to the rag. The dog must use its nose to find the rag. After the dog finds that smell, the trainer hides things with the same smell. The dog gets a treat each time it finds the right smell.

Dogs are called "man's best friend." It is good to know their noses can help us!

Follow Your Nose, Dog! **31**

Follow Your Nose, Dog! (continued)

Comprehension Activity

Write your answers to the questions on the lines.

1 Name two jobs dogs can do.

Ideas: find people, sniff out cancer

2 Why are dogs better at some jobs than people are?

Idea: Dogs have a much better sense of smell.

3 In a few sentences, explain how dogs can be trained.

Idea: The dogs are trained by playing with a rag that has a smell. Then the rag is hidden and the dog is asked to find it so the dog gets used to trying to find that smell.

4 What other job do you think a dog might be trained to do? Tell why a dog's sense of smell would help it do that job.

Answers will vary.

32 *Follow Your Nose, Dog!*

| fence | Harry | melon | Willa |

Watch That Melon

Willa and her little brother Harry ran to the garden. They could not wait to see if the melons in their garden were ready to eat.

Willa stepped over the fence and then lifted Harry into the garden. "Look!" Willa said. Under the green leaves was a melon! Willa bent down to look closer and saw three bites in the melon. Willa called to her dad. "Look, Dad. Something has eaten our melon!"

"How could an animal get into the garden? We have this fence," Dad said when he saw the melon.

"We will stop whoever is doing this," Willa said. She looked at three more little melons with small bites. "I'll watch them all day!"

Willa and Harry took turns watching the melons. How slowly they were growing! Still, each day, the melons got a little bigger. As Willa and Harry watched the plants, they saw a toad inside the fence, and they saw bugs on the leaves, but they didn't see anything that could eat their melons.

Then one morning, Willa saw something hop in the grass outside the garden. A rabbit moved closer to the fence, found a hole, and slipped under it. It was going to eat their melons. "Mom, Dad, Harry," Willa yelled. "Come see this!"

They all came running. Mom got to the fence just in time to see the rabbit hop away. "Oh, no you don't," Mom said.

"I'll make a better fence," said Dad, and he fixed all the holes.

When the fence was fixed, there were no more rabbits in the garden. When the leaves turned brown, the melons were ready. Willa picked the biggest melon. "Now we can be the ones to eat the melons." It was the best melon Willa, Harry, Dad, and Mom had ever eaten!

Watch That Melon **33**

Watch That Melon (continued)

Comprehension Activities

Write the answers to the questions on the lines.

1 What is the problem for the family in this story?

Idea: The problem is that something is eating the melons

2 How is the problem in the story solved?

Idea: Willa watches the garden until she sees a rabbit enter the garden. Then Dad fixes the fence.

3 What kinds of animals do Willa and Harry see in and around their garden?

Ideas: a toad, bugs, a rabbit.

4 Put the events of the story in order by writing 1, 2, 3 and 4.

2 Willa and Harry take turns watching the melons.

4 Willa's family eats the melon

3 Willa sees the rabbit.

1 Willa finds a melon with bites in it.

34 *Watch That Melon*

| grade | invention | inventor | tubes | Rodney |

Rodney, the Inventor Who Never Gave Up

Rodney was an inventor. His newest invention was a backpack on wheels. It had a motor and moved by itself. It carried his books, pens, paper, and lunch. Rodney was sure that everybody in his third-grade class would want one.

But things didn't turn out like he'd planned. When Rodney took his backpack invention to school, it was a big mess. It bumped into students. It crashed into his teacher.

"Stop that thing!" called his teacher, Ms. Green.

Rodney picked up his backpack. "A good inventor never gives up," he said. "And I, Rodney, will never give up."

Soon Rodney had another idea. He made an invention to help Ms. Green pass back homework. Rodney opened a latch on the box. "You put the homework in here," he says as he showed Ms. Green the box. "And the homework comes out here."

Rodney pressed a button and a sheet of homework shot across the room. Then all the other papers went flying up into the air. It took a long time to clean them up! Ms. Green was not happy. "A good inventor never gives up," Rodney said.

One day, Rodney said, "I've made the best invention of my life." The class groaned.

"What does it do?" asked Ms. Green, trying to smile.

"It will clean our room," Rodney said. He showed the class his invention. It was a tall box. "Watch," said Rodney. He reached into the box and the box began to shake. Someone yelled, but Rodney smiled. Soon the shaking stopped. Rodney moved the box and under it was a broom!

"Do you like my invention?" Rodney asked.

"We like this new invention," Ms. Green said, and everybody laughed.

"A good inventor never gives up," Rodney said.

Rodney, the Inventor Who Never Gave Up (continued)

Comprehension Activities

Write the answers to the questions on the lines.

1 Why does Rodney say he keeps making new inventions?

Idea: Rodney says a good inventor never gives up.

2 What is Rodney's problem in this story?

Idea: The problem is that Rodney's inventions do not work and his teacher and classmates are not happy with him.

3 How are Rodney's backpack invention and homework invention alike?

Ideas: Both could be used at school. Both made a big mess.

Rodney, the Inventor Who Never Gave Up (continued)

4 What would you like to invent? What will it do?

Answers will vary.

_____

_____

_____

Draw a picture of your invention.

Drawings will vary.

| desert | pouch |

The Red Kangaroo

Many different kinds of animals live in the hot, dry desert. Small animals find shade from the hot sun by hiding under the ground. Birds can fly away when it is too hot, but how do the big animals live? Red kangaroos have found many ways to "beat the heat."

Like other big desert animals, kangaroos sleep in the hot hours of the day and are awake when the sun goes down. At night, they look for grass and plants to eat. They look for water to drink. Sometimes, there is little to drink in the desert. Red kangaroos can live with no water for a long time if they have green grass to eat. A red kangaroo has a body that can hold water.

Kangaroos are able to go far to look for food and water. Red kangaroos can hop as fast as 30 miles per hour. They can go a long way with each hop. Did you know that kangaroos can hop, but they can't walk? Their back legs must always move together, not one at a time. To go slow, the kangaroos lean on their tails and front feet. Then they swing their back legs across and back.

When a baby kangaroo is born, it is very small. It lives in its mother's pouch. There, it drinks its mother's milk and keeps growing. After just over 30 weeks in the pouch, the baby is ready to come out. It begins to look around. Soon it will hop through the desert on its own legs.

Comprehension Activities

Write the answers to the questions on the lines.

1 What are two ways red kangaroos "beat the heat" in the desert?

Ideas: They sleep during the day and come out at night when it is cooler. They can go for a long time without drinking water.

2 It is easy for a kangaroo to go fast but hard for it to go slow. Why is this?

Ideas: Its back legs do not move one at a time, so it can hop but not walk. It has to swing its back legs back and forth to go slow.

The Red Kangaroo (continued)

3 Where do baby kangaroos live until they are big enough to hop around?

They live in their mother's pouch.

Think of a different animal. Then write the answer to the question on the lines.

4 What kind of animal did you think of?

Answers will vary. Accept reasonable responses.

5 What are two ways your animal and the kangaroo are the *same*?

Answers will vary. Accept reasonable responses.

6 What are two ways your animal and the kangaroo are *different*?

Answers will vary. Accept reasonable responses.

Dr. Art Kramer	professor	psychology	researcher

Fit Body, Fit Mind

Most of us know that exercise can help keep our bodies fit. Do you know that exercise is good for our minds, too? Exercising can help us think clearly. It can also help us feel happy.

Dr. Art Kramer is a professor of psychology. He teaches about the brain and how it works. He is a researcher, too. He seeks answers to questions. He wanted to know what exercise can do for people's brains. In his research, he asked some people to exercise a lot. He asked others not to exercise at all. Then he tested the people. The tests would help him know how clearly they could think. Dr. Kramer's tests showed him that those who exercised did better on the tests. Exercise helped people to think more clearly.

Dr. Kramer also found that exercise helps older people. It helps them think more clearly. Parts of the brain can get smaller as people get older. This can make it harder to think clearly. When people exercise, these parts of the brain do not get as small. Older people who exercised did better on the tests.

Did you know that exercise can help us feel happy? Researchers say it can. People who were sad said exercise helped them to feel less sad. It is good to know that being fit can help you smile!

What does all of this mean? It means that we should exercise for a fit body and a fit mind. We should walk, run, or swim to help both our body and our mind!

Comprehension Activity

Write your answers to the questions on the lines.

1 What are three ways exercise can help you?

Idea: It can help you think more clearly, feel happier, and keep your body fit.

2 How can exercise help older people?

Idea: Exercise helps prevent parts of the brain of older people from getting smaller and helps people think clearly.

Fit Body, Fit Mind (continued)

3 How does Dr. Kramer know that exercise helps people to think more clearly?

Idea: Dr. Kramer did testing. In the tests, some people exercised often and others did not. Then he gave tests to all the people. Those who exercised did better on tests. This showed that they could think more clearly.

4 What form of exercise do you like? How do you feel after you exercise?

Answers will vary.

---

double	glared	nickname	practice	worried

Lady Baseball

"Third out!" Meg called, holding up the baseball after her diving catch. Meg ran in and the other team glared at her as they passed. Meg was not only the best baseball player on her team, she was also the only girl on the team.

Even the newest player, Tim, gave Meg a sharp look as he popped her a high five. "Not bad for a girl," he said.

"A lady, you mean," said Meg.

"Yeah, Lady Baseball," he snapped.

As she walked home, Meg talked to her best friend Sara. "Those boys are upset because you're so good," she told Meg with a small smile.

"I know," Meg said. "It would be more fun if we all could be friends."

The next day, Sara, who was sick a lot, was not at school again. Meg began to worry, because Sara seemed so tired all the time. Meg hoped that there wasn't anything wrong.

At baseball practice, Meg dropped an easy fly ball, struck out, and later fell while running to first base. Tim helped her up.

"What's wrong?" he asked.

Meg kicked the dirt and said, "Sara's sick again."

The next time Meg was at bat, Tim yelled, "Go, Lady Baseball!" Meg couldn't help but smile at that, and when other players yelled it too, Meg hit a double. It made her feel good to hear them cheer.

The next day, just before the baseball game, Tim asked Meg about Sara. "I talked with her last night," Meg said, "and she will soon be back at school. The doctor says she is going to be fine."

"I'm glad," said Tim. "Let's play ball."

Meg started to think about baseball and everyone cheered when Lady Baseball made a diving catch to win the game.

Lady Baseball (continued)

Comprehension Activity

Write the answers to the questions on the lines.

1 At the beginning of the story, why are the boys upset with Meg?

Idea: She is a better baseball player than they are, and they are jealous.

2 Why does Meg play badly at baseball practice?

Idea: Her friend Sara is sick, and Meg is worried about her.

3 Tim calls Meg "Lady Baseball." How does he use the nickname the first time he says it? How does he use the nickname later?

Idea: At first, Tim uses the nickname in a mean, taunting way. Later, he uses the nickname in a nice, supportive way.

| buzzed | classmates | joked | weekend |

A New Start

Linda woke up before her clock buzzed. She was upset. It was her first day at a new school, and she did not know what it would be like.

Linda's family had just moved to a new town. Linda was upset about leaving her school, friends, and home behind. Her mom got a new job, so the family moved right away. Linda was unhappy about not ending third grade with her friends.

While her dad drove Linda to school, she talked about all of the questions she had. How would she find her classroom? Would she make new friends?

When she got to the school, a teacher walked Linda to Mrs. Smith's classroom. "This is Mrs. Smith's classroom. I'm glad you're here," said Mrs. Smith.

"Thank you," Linda said.

Just then, the bell rang and Linda's new classmates began coming in. Linda felt upset again. Would her classmates like her? Would she be eating lunch alone?

It turned out that Linda's desk was right next to Tina's. Tina came over to Linda right away and told Linda the names of all the kids in the class.

At lunch time, Linda felt too shy to ask Tina to eat with her. Before Linda could worry much about it, Tina saw Linda. She asked Linda to have lunch with her. While they ate, Linda and Tina talked and joked like they had been friends for ages!

At the end of the day, Tina asked Linda to come to her house. She was hoping that Linda's mom and dad would let her come over that weekend.

When Linda met her dad outside, he asked, "How was your first day?"

Linda smiled and said, "It was fun, Dad! I made a new friend! I don't know what I was so scared about!"

A New Start (continued)

Comprehension Activity

Circle the letter of the best answer for each question.

1 Why was Linda feeling scared?
   a. She woke up too early for school.
   b. It was the last day of school.
   c. It was the first day at a new school.

2 What happened when Linda walked into the lunchroom?
   a. Tina asked Linda to have lunch with her.
   b. Linda found a spot to sit down alone.
   c. Tina laughed at Linda.

3 From what you read, how do you think Linda felt at the end of the day?
   a. sad
   b. happy
   c. scared

| area | field | recycling | sign | Yama |

Making a Difference

Bill, Yama, and Jack were best friends. The three boys did everything together. On the way home from school one day, they were talking about their field trip and recycling. They saw how easy it was to recycle things like cans, paper, and glass.

Yama said, "It's too bad we don't have a way to recycle around here. We would have less litter on the streets."

Jack added, "It would make the area cleaner."

Bill snapped his fingers and said, "I've got it! We can start a recycling group! I'll bet my dad will let us pick up cans and paper in front of his store!"

The boys talked to Bill's father about their plan, and he said it was a good idea. With the help of their families, the boys used wood and nails given by a store owner to make a recycling bin.

Bill's father let the boys make a sign about the new recycling bin for his store window. A few people began dropping off paper and cans in the bin. Bill, Yama, and Jack asked the other store owners if they could make signs for their stores, too. They all said yes.

The boys sorted the recycling bin every few days, and Bill's father would drive them to the recycling site to drop off the cans and paper.

People liked to recycle. They saw that since people started recycling, there was not as much litter on the sidewalks. The boys took the money they got from recycling and planted flowers in big pots outside of each store on the block. Their hard work made it a nicer area for everyone to live.

Making a Difference (continued)

Comprehension Activity

Circle the letter of the best answer for each question.

1 Why did the boys want to start recycling?
   a. to clean up the area
   b. to make money
   c. it was their homework

2 What happened just after the boys made the recycling bin?
   a. They planted flowers.
   b. They talked about the field trip.
   c. They made a sign.

3 What was the outcome of recycling in the story?
   a. The area was cleaner.
   b. The boys had fun.
   c. The boys worked together.

Learn About Words

Underline the nouns and circle the verb.

1 Bill talked to his father.

2 People filled the recycling bin.

3 Everyone likes the new flowers.

America	Appaloosa	Native American	Morgan	soldiers

Horses of America

Explorers came to America in the 1500s. They brought horses with them. They explored America on horseback. Some horses got away. Many free horses were born.

Native Americans found a use for these horses. They rode them to hunt for food. They used horses to carry goods. They used horses to move their homes from place to place. Native Americans took good care of their horses.

People in America found horses to be helpful. They trained horses to pull carts. They trained them to help with the farming. Ranchers rode horses to move herds of cows. Horses were used to help build railroads. Soldiers moved around on horseback. Horses helped with many jobs in America.

Today, horses still work. Officers in cities ride horses. People ride horses where cars cannot go. Ranchers use horses for herding. People also ride horses for fun and exercise.

You can find horses in sport, too. The sport is horse racing. Some horses run short races. Others run long races. In some races, the horses jump over fences. People also show horses. The best-looking horse wins first prize.

Caring for horses is a big job. They need exercise every day. They need good food to eat. Horses must be brushed. Their stalls must be kept clean.

There are many kinds of horses. There are Morgans, Appaloosas, and others. The Morgan is good for riding and pulling carts. The Appaloosa is a strong horse for doing work. In the West, wild horses still run free.

Horses of America (continued)

Comprehension Activities

Circle the letter of the best answer for each question.

1 Which job is one that a horse might do?
   a. help pick crops by hand
   b. help move heavy things
   c. help write a story

2 Which three things do horses need?
   a. exercise, good food, clean stalls
   b. a race, a cart, horseshoes
   c. a job, exercise, a place to run free

3 How did horses help Native Americans?
   a. Horses helped them pull carts.
   b. Horses helped them hunt.
   c. Horses helped them build railroads.

Learn About Words

In the sentences below, circle the adjectives that go with the underlined nouns.

1 The horse pulled the heavy cart.

2 I saw a tall horse.

3 That horse has black hair.

---

apartment	blanket	clues	Strawberry	wrote

The Case of the Missing Bear

Chad was three years old. He had a soft red teddy bear named Strawberry. Strawberry was his best buddy, and Chad couldn't sleep without him.

One day after lunch, Chad couldn't find Strawberry. He looked all over his room. He asked his brother Mike if he had seen Strawberry.

"No, I haven't seen Strawberry today," said Mike. Chad got upset.

"I can't find him!" he sobbed.

"Let me help you," said Mike. "We can crack the case of the missing teddy bear!"

Mike got a pen and paper to write down clues. He asked, "Where did you last see Strawberry?"

Chad answered, "He was on my bed this morning."

"Who could have moved Strawberry?" asked Mike.

"Mom could have washed him. He was a little dirty," said Chad. "Dad could have put him in the kitchen. Strawberry likes to help Dad make dinner."

Mike wrote down the clues. First, they asked their mom if she took Strawberry to wash him.

She said that she hadn't seen Strawberry all day. Then they asked their dad if he had Strawberry. He said he didn't know where Strawberry was.

Mike took his mom and dad off his list. Then he had a super idea! Mike said they could go to all the spots that Chad went that day to try to find the bear.

First, the boys checked Chad's bed. They took off all the blankets, but there was no Strawberry. Next, they went to the kitchen. They peeked under chairs and tables, but no Strawberry. They looked around the apartment, but did not find Strawberry.

Just when Chad was afraid he had lost Strawberry for good, he remembered that he went to his friend's apartment to play after lunch. Chad and Mike ran out into the hallway. There on the floor was Strawberry!

Chad picked his bear up and gave him a squeeze! Chad thanked Mike for helping him find Strawberry. Chad and Mike took Strawberry to Chad's room and tucked him into bed.

Name _____ Date _____

The Case of the Missing Bear (continued)

Comprehension Activity

Circle A, B, or C.

1 What was Chad missing?
a. his stuffed dog
b. his teddy bear
c. his blanket

2 Why do you think Mike wrote down the clues?
a. so he could remember them all
b. so he could write a story about them
c. so he could tell his mom and dad about them

3 Where was Strawberry found?
a. in the kitchen
b. in Chad's bed
c. in the hallway

Learn About Words

Circle the verb in each sentence.

1 The teddy bear **fell** on the floor.

2 Chad **cried** about Strawberry.

3 Mike and Chad **cheered**.

4 Mike **wrote** down the clues.

5 They **looked** around the apartment

Name _____ Date _____

Antarctica	dolphins	penguin	scientists

Antarctica

Pack your warmest clothes! You're going on a trip. You are going to Antarctica! "Where is that?" you ask. Antarctica is the continent that is the farthest south. It's a long plane ride away. It will take many hours to go that far south. Your plane may have to make a few stops along the way.

You have heard of the North Pole. You know it is very cold there. Do you know where the South Pole is? The South Pole is in Antarctica. It is very cold there, too. It is almost covered with ice. Most of the ice found in the world is in and around Antarctica. It is the coldest and windiest place on

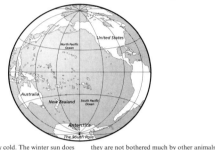

Earth! Winters are very cold. The winter sun does not rise for about six months. This makes winter very dark all day. The sun shines almost all day in the summer. It is still cold in the summer. It never gets warm enough to melt much of the ice.

Not many people live in Antarctica. Even fewer people stay during the winter months. Scientists from all over the world go to Antarctica. They go to learn about the land, plants, and

animals. These scientists stay indoors most of the time.

There is land under the ice of Antarctica. Not much is known about the land. Scientists do know that there are mountains under the ice. Some of the mountains were made by ice rubbing against rock. Not many plants can live in Antarctica. In some places, you won't find any plants at all. You could not have a garden in Antarctica!

You won't find many animals there. One animal you will find is a penguin. Penguins can live in Antarctica because they like the cold. Also, they are not bothered much by other animals. Penguins have a layer of fat. It helps to keep them warm. They can keep warm in very cold water. Other animals live around Antarctica. Seals, fish, and dolphins are able to live in the cold water around this very cold continent.

Name _____ Date _____

Antarctica (continued)

Comprehension Activities

Circle the letter of the best answer for each question.

1 Which sentence would be the best topic sentence for this passage, the sentence that tells what the passage is about?
a. Antarctica is a cold place.
b. Antarctica is not an easy place to live.
c. Penguins live in Antarctica.

2 Why doesn't the ice on Antarctica melt in the summer?
a. It is too windy.
b. The sun doesn't rise.
c. It never gets warm enough.

3 What helps penguins stay warm in cold areas?
a. their wings
b. a layer of fat
c. a nest

Learn About Words

For each word below, circle the letter for the word with the opposite meaning.

1 cold
a. chilly
b. hot
c. cool

2 south
a. east
b. west
c. north

3 under
a. below
b. over
c. away

Name _____ Date _____

favorite	Jessica	picnic	promised

Sledding with Grandpa

It was a Saturday morning. Jessica was up, dressed, and ready to go. She was waiting for her grandfather's car to pull up. It had snowed during the night, and a beautiful white blanket of snow covered the ground.

Once a month, Jessica's grandfather would take her out for the day. Jessica looked forward to their special Saturdays together. They would talk on the phone to plan their time together. They always chose to do something fun. One day last summer, they took a picnic to the beach and went swimming. Last fall they picked apples. On this winter day, they were going sledding.

Grandpa pulled into the driveway. Jessica helped him strap the sled on top of his car. They both hopped into the car like excited children.

Grandpa and Jessica drove to the sledding hill where he used to take Jessica's father when he was young. Grandpa said some of his happiest moments were on this sledding hill. Grandpa pulled the sled up to the top of the hill. Jessica was afraid of going down the hill too fast, so Grandpa

got on the sled behind her. He promised that he would slow the sled down if it went too fast.

Down the hill they went! Jessica was not afraid at all. She laughed when the snow sprayed in her face at the bottom of the hill. Grandpa laughed too.

Grandpa and Jessica slid down the hill again and again. They slid down a different way each time. Sometimes Jessica rode in front of Grandpa. Sometimes she rode behind Grandpa. Once they tried to go backwards. Another time, they tried to go sideways. That time they landed face-first in the snow! Their faces were wet, but they were laughing!

After that, Jessica and Grandpa went to Grandpa's house to warm up. Grandpa made lunch. He made Jessica's favorite soup. While they ate, Grandpa told stories about sledding many years ago. He and Jessica's dad used to slide down the same hill. Jessica said that when she grows up, she will tell her own stories about sledding with Grandpa.

Sledding with Grandpa (continued)

Comprehension Activity

Circle the letter of the best answer for each question.

1 How often did Jessica have a special day with Grandpa?
 a. once a week
 b. once a month ⟵
 c. once a year

2 Why did Grandpa pick that sledding hill?
 a. It was the hill where he took Jessica's dad. ⟵
 b. It was the nearest hill.
 c. It was the best hill for sledding.

3 What happened when Grandpa and Jessica went down the hill sideways?
 a. They made it all the way to the bottom of the hill.
 b. They landed face-first in the snow. ⟵
 c. They met Jessica's dad at the bottom of the hill.

Learn About Words

One good way to learn words is to use them. Look at the number at the end of each sentence. Find the paragraph in the story with the same number. Then find the best word to fill the blank. Write the word.

1 _____Sledding_____ is a winter activity you can do in the snow. (2)

2 Grandpa had many happy ____moments____ sledding with Jessica's father. (4)

3 Jessica laughed as snow ____sprayed____ in her face the first time she went down the hill. (5)

Sledding with Grandpa   55

---

aunt	fields	invited	surprise

Carl's Summer on the Farm

It was the last day of school, and Carl was looking forward to spending his summer playing with his friends. They had planned a lot of fun things to do. That night, Carl's mom said, "I have a surprise for you. Your Uncle Bill and Aunt Fern have invited you to spend the summer with them on their farm."

The next day, Carl's mom drove him to the farm. Carl missed his friends already. His mom kept telling him that he would have a great time on the farm, but Carl was not so sure.

The first night on the farm, Carl realized how quiet it was. He didn't hear any of the usual city noise. It was so quiet that it was hard for Carl to sleep. In the morning, Uncle Bill woke Carl up very early, saying, "It's time to milk the cows." Carl couldn't believe that he had to do chores.

That first day on the farm was very hard. First Carl helped Uncle Bill take care of the animals,

and then he helped Aunt Fern weed the garden. After supper, they sat outside and ate Aunt Fern's ice cream. They talked a bit and listened to the soft sounds of evening.

Carl quickly got used to life on the farm. After the chores were done, there was time for fun. Some days they would go swimming in the river, or Carl would take long bike rides along the dirt roads. On other days, Carl and his aunt would go bird-watching. Carl even began to like doing his chores! He talked to the animals while he fed them, and he and his uncle told silly jokes as they worked in the fields. Carl never laughed so hard in his life.

The summer went by very quickly. When he got back to the city, Carl was surprised at how noisy it was. He missed his aunt and uncle and all of the animals on the farm. It felt good to be home, but Carl hoped that he could spend next summer on the farm again.

Comprehension Activity

Circle the letter of the best answer for each question.

1 Which word best tells how Carl first felt about the idea of going to a farm?
 a. unhappy ⟵
 b. pleased
 c. afraid

2 What did Carl learn in this story?
 a. You can't have fun without your friends.
 b. The city is the best place to live.
 c. It can be fun to try new things. ⟵

3 When Carl returned home at the end of the summer, why did he think the city was noisy?
 a. He was used to the quiet at the farm. ⟵
 b. The city had changed while he was away.
 c. His friends said it was too noisy.

56   *Carl's Summer on the Farm*

Carl's Summer on the Farm (continued)

Learn About Words

For each word below, circle the letter for the word with the opposite meaning.

1 awake
 a. up
 b. happy
 c. asleep ⟵

2 friendly
 a. nice
 b. mean ⟵
 c. kind

3 stand
 a. step
 b. walk
 c. sit ⟵

Carl's Summer on the Farm   57

Thomas Edison	lightbulb	machine	phonograph	record

Thomas Edison

Thomas Edison lived from 1847 until 1931. As a child, he did not go to school for very long. Instead, his mother and father were his teachers. He liked to read and find out about things. He liked to try new ideas. He would invent things to help make people's lives better or more fun.

Somebody else had made a new tool called a telephone. Edison's ears did not work very well. It was hard for him to hear a voice on the telephone. He found a way to make the sound louder. The tool Edison made is still used in telephones today. Without Thomas Edison, you might not be able to hear the other person when you answer the telephone.

Of all the new tools Edison made, one of the most important is the phonograph. Edison's phonograph was the first tool that could record a sound and play it back. The first phonograph worked with the help of some tinfoil. When you

hear a CD or listen to voice mail, you can thank Thomas Edison!

Thomas Edison did not make the first lightbulb. He did make the first lightbulb that would stay lit for many hours! It was the first lightbulb that could light homes for many hours.

How would power for the lightbulbs get to the homes? Edison had the answer. He found a way to bring power to many homes all at once. Without Edison's ideas, you might still need a fire to see at night!

Have you watched a movie lately? Thank Thomas Edison! He was one of the first makers of moving pictures. Now we call them "movies." He made a machine to take the movies. He made another machine to show the movies.

Thomas Edison was always looking for new ways of doing things. His ideas have made our lives better and more fun.

Comprehension Activity

Circle the letter of the best answer for each question.

1 What is this story about?
 a. When Thomas Edison was a child
 b. Thomas Edison's mother and father
 c. Things that Thomas Edison invented ⟵

2 How was Edison's telephone better than the first telephones?
 a. It was louder. ⟵
 b. It was easy to use.
 c. It did not need a wire.

3 What could happen because of Thomas Edison's lightbulb?
 a. People could see at night.
 b. Light could be used outside.
 c. Lights could stay lit a long time ⟵

58   *Thomas Edison*

Thomas Edison (continued)

Learn About Words

Look at these word parts and what they mean:

| graph – writing, recording | micro – small | phone, phono – sound | tele – far, distant |

Now look at these words. Use the word parts to figure out what they mean.

| microphone | phonograph | telegraph | telephone |

Write each word by its meaning.

❶ machine that records sound _____ *phonograph*

❷ machine that writes far away _____ *telegraph*

❸ machine that takes sound far away _____ *telephone*

❹ machine that takes a small sound and makes it bigger _____ *microphone*

| Mercury | Venus | Mars | Jupiter | Saturn | Uranus |
| | Neptune | Pluto | dwarf | | |

The Planets in Our Solar System

Earth is just one of eight planets in a huge group. All of the planets move around the sun. Mercury, Venus, Earth, and Mars are all rocky planets. Jupiter, Saturn, Uranus, and Neptune are made mostly of gases.

Mercury is closest to the sun, so it can get hotter there than any other planet. Because it doesn't have any air to hold heat in, it can get very cold at night.

The next planet is Venus. Venus has thick clouds around it that keep heat inside, so it is hot. Sunlight bounces off the clouds, making Venus visible from Earth.

Earth is the third planet from the sun. Much of Earth is covered by water. Earth has four seasons because of the way it spins as it moves around the sun.

Mars is the next planet. Special robots have landed on Mars and found proof of water there. If there is or once was water on Mars, there could be some living things on Mars that we have not found yet.

Jupiter is the next planet, and it is the largest. It is more like a large, hot star than a planet, and it would be a star if it were much larger. Jupiter has 63 moons, more than any other planet.

Saturn has rings around it. Scientists think these rings are made of water and ice. The winds on Saturn are very fast, making Saturn look like a striped planet.

The next planet is Uranus. It is so far from the sun that it takes 84 years to go around the Sun once. Each season on Uranus is 20 years long.

Neptune is the farthest planet from the sun. You need special tools to see it because it is so far away. It takes 165 years for Neptune to go around the sun.

What about Pluto? Until 2006, Pluto was thought to be the farthest planet from the sun. Scientists decided to change the definition of a planet, so Pluto is now called a dwarf planet. The more scientists study the planets, the more they learn about them.

The Planets in Our Solar System (continued)

Comprehension Activity

Circle the letter of the best answer for each question.

❶ Which planet is closest to the sun?
   a. Jupiter
   b. Mercury
   c. Earth

❷ Which sentence best tells the main idea of this passage?
   a. Neptune is the farthest planet from the sun.
   b. Planets move around the sun.
   c. Eight planets move around our sun.

❸ Which sentence best describes Earth?
   a. Earth, like Pluto, is far from the sun.
   b. Earth is a rocky planet covered mostly by water.
   c. Earth is a large planet made up of many gases.

Learn About Words

You can often tell the meaning of a word by reading the words around it. Find the word in the story that matches the definition. The paragraph number in parentheses will help you find the word. Then write the word after its definition.

❶ objects in space that move around the sun (1) _____ *planets*

❷ spring, summer, winter, fall (4) _____ *seasons*

❸ not a planet, not a moon, but a very large, hot object in space (6) _____ *star*

| beachcombing | parents | speckled |

Beachcombing

A large, gray beach house stands on the white sands of the beach right beside the sea. Outside the open window of the house, the early morning sky slowly grows. The sound of waves crashing softly on the shore is joined by the sharp cry of sea birds. Inside, three children stir in their beds, opening their eyes. Emma, Rose, and Jake dash to the window and sniff the salt air.

"Come on," Rose says. "Let's get Mom and Dad. I want to go out and play on the beach."

"Me too!" shout Emma and Jake. "Wake up, Mom and Dad, and let's go beachcombing!"

While their parents yawn, the three children jump into their clothes and grab their pails for the beach. The front door flies open and bare feet hurry across the smooth boards of the old, worn deck. The whole family runs together, laughing, from the deck across the sand toward the foaming waves. The water feels warm as it washes over their legs and the children run back and forth, chasing the waves for a few minutes. Then Rose comes running to her parents, holding a speckled shell in her small, wet fingers.

"What is this, Mom?" she asks her mother.

"That's a seashell, Rose," says Mom. "Hold it to your ear, and tell me if you can you hear the sound of the sea."

The three children take turns holding the shell to their ears as they listen to the whisper that sounds like the roaring of the sea. Rose listens one last time before she puts the shell in her pail.

"Let's go find some more shells!" shouts Emma.

The children dash around the beach, picking up shells of different colors and shapes. They find white shells and yellow ones, brown shells and gold ones. Some shells are large and speckled, while others are tiny and pale. Some shells are covered with sharp little points, while others feel smooth like glass. Soon all three pails are filled with many kinds of shells. The shells spill over the tops until the pails are almost—but not quite—too heavy for the children to carry.

Tired but happy, Emma, Rose, and Jake dance across the hot sand and back to the beach house. They will spend their afternoon sitting on the beach-house deck, sorting and counting their treasures from the sea.

Comprehension Activities

Circle the letter of the best answer for each question.

❶ Where is the family in this story taking a vacation?
   a. at the beach
   b. in the desert
   c. in the mountains

❷ What are the children in the story doing?
   a. climbing trees
   b. playing volleyball
   c. looking for seashells

Beachcombing (continued)

3 How do Emma, Rose, and Jake feel at the beginning of the story?
a. afraid
b. hungry
c. excited

4 Why do the children hold the shell to their ears?
a. to feel how heavy it is
b. to hear the sound it makes
c. to empty the sand out of it

Write the answers to the questions on the lines.

5 What are three sounds that people hear in the story?

Ideas: talking, laughter, waves, birds, shells

6 What does "treasures from the sea" mean at the very end of the story?

Idea: "Treasures from the sea" are the shells the children collected.

7 What are three different ways the children could sort their shells?

Ideas: by size, color, shape

---

fir	forester	logger	moss

At Work in the Forest

Hi! I'm a forester. My name is Jenny, and my job is to take care of the forest. The forest is an important and wonderful place. Come along with me and I will show you why! It's a very nice morning as we set out to learn about the forest. The bright smell of pine and fir greets our noses,

and a blazing, blue sky lights the tops of the trees. Along the path are patches of soft, green moss. Flowers line the trail, adding their own sweet smell to the summer air. Birds sing above us, and a squirrel barks at us from the top of a tall tree.

Soon, another sound reaches our ears. Shouts and laughter float on the breeze and a motor hums to life. Men are at work in the forest with big saws! These men are called loggers. They cut down trees, nip off the branches, and load the logs into trucks. The trucks carry the logs down the mountain to the mill, where the logs will be cut into boards. My job is to help the loggers decide which trees to cut down.

We leave the loggers and go a little farther on the mountain road, where we come to another group of people working. Instead of cutting down trees, these people plant new trees! This part of the forest was burned in a fire a few years ago, and the workers are planting trees to take the place of those that burned. These people also plant trees in areas where the trees have been cut down by loggers. To plant a tree, the worker swings a heavy tool, making a hole in the hard soil. Working fast, he pulls a tiny baby tree from the heavy bag on his belt and sticks it quickly into the hole. The worker will plant many hundreds of trees today. Before long, a new forest will grow from the ashes of the old.

Our forests give us wood to build our homes, schools, and stores. They give us good places to camp, walk, and fish. I am proud of the important work I do, helping to take care of our forests. Maybe someday you will want to go to work in the forest, too!

At Work in the Forest (continued)

Comprehension Activity

Circle the letter of the best answer for each question.

1 The person who is telling this story works
a. on a ship.
b. in a forest.
c. in an office.

2 At the mill in the story, the trees are cut into
a. paper.
b. boards.
c. branches.

3 Part of the forest is in ashes because of
a. a fire.
b. a strong wind.
c. road construction.

Learn About Words

Many job names end with *-er*. Write the name of the person that does each job.

1 Cuts down trees for logs _____ logger

2 Plants new trees _____ (tree) planter

3 Takes care of the forest _____ forester

---

bravery	caught	chewed	climbed	lion

The Lion and the Mouse

One day, a lion was sleeping in the tall grass, when a tiny mouse decided to have some fun. The mouse began running all over the lion's back!

The lion felt a tickle on his back and sat up suddenly. The mouse froze, hoping the lion wouldn't spot him. The lion turned his head and was shocked to see a mouse standing on his back.

The mouse tried to run away, but when he did, the lion placed his big paw on the mouse's tail. Although the mouse was small, the lion was really hungry. He leaned over to eat the mouse.

When he realized that he was about to be eaten, the mouse said, "Wait, great lion." The lion was stunned to meet a mouse who was so brave to talk to him.

The lion asked, "What do you want?"

The mouse cried, "Please, lion, if you let me go, I will never forget it."

The lion laughed. "Why should I let you go? Why should I care about what you think?"

"If you let me go, maybe I will be able to do something nice for you in return someday," said the mouse.

The lion laughed so loudly that the ground shook. "What can a tiny mouse do for a great lion?" But he was stunned by the mouse's bravery, so he let the mouse go.

A few days later, the lion was caught in a hunter's trap. The hunter wanted to take the lion to the king as a gift, so he went to get his wagon. The hunter left the lion tied to a tree.

The lion was not able to get away. While he sat there feeling sorry for himself, the tiny mouse happened to walk by. "What happened to you?" asked the mouse.

"I got caught in a hunter's trap. Now he's going to take me to the king, and who knows what will happen to me there," said the lion sadly.

The mouse remembered how the lion had let him go. He wasn't going to forget how kind the lion had been to him. So the mouse climbed up on the lion's back. He chewed on the rope that kept the lion tied to the tree. Finally, he chewed all the way through and freed the lion. The lion was thankful that the mouse saved his life, and they became friends forever.

The Lion and the Mouse (continued)

Comprehension Activity

Circle the letter of the best answer for each question.

1 Which character helps the other first in this story?
- a. the lion
- b. the mouse
- c. the hunter

2 In what way are the mouse and the lion in this story like people?
- a. They chew ropes.
- b. They roar.
- c. They talk.

3 Which sentence best tells the lesson learned in this story?
- a. Little friends can be good friends.
- b. Always trust a mouse.
- c. Lions always get away.

Learn About Words

Read each sentence from the story. Then choose the two words that combine to make the underlined contraction in the sentence.

1 Now he's going to take me to the king.
- a. he sees
- b. he was
- c. he is

2 He wasn't going to forget how kind the lion had been to him.
- a. was not
- b. were not
- c. will not

3 The mouse froze, hoping the lion wouldn't spot him.
- a. was not
- b. would not
- c. would have

| awards | concert | donated | musicians | Roberta Guaspari | violin |

The Music of Life

Roberta Guaspari is a music teacher in New York City. She teaches the violin to children. She teaches in the part of the city called Harlem. Harlem is a poorer part of New York City. When she started teaching in the 1980s, there was not much music in the schools.

Ms. Guaspari loved the children. She loved teaching music. The children loved learning music. They loved learning to play the violin. But in 1991, New York City schools had no money for the music program. Ms. Guaspari was afraid she would no longer have a job.

She wanted to save the music program. She wanted to keep the music alive in the schools. She wrote letters to everyone she thought could help. Then a story about her students was in the New York Times newspaper. She also told her story on TV.

People were interested in her work. Her violin students performed in a concert. They called the concert of violins Fiddlefest. Well-known musicians came to the concert. They wanted to hear the students play. They liked what they heard. The musicians donated their time and money so the students could have music lessons. They asked others to give money.

They raised enough money to keep the school music program going. Ms. Guaspari also opened a music center. At the center, students learn to play the violin even if they cannot pay for lessons.

Ms. Guaspari knows music makes a difference for children. Music students do better in school. They make something delightful with their music. This makes them proud. It makes them feel good. The music students have played for Presidents. They have played in movies. They have been on TV. They have traveled far to other countries to play music. They have played with well-known musicians.

Ms. Guaspari wrote a book. It is about her life and her work. The book is called *Music of the Heart.* Her story was made into two movies. The movies are *Small Wonders* and *Music of the Heart.*

Ms. Guaspari has earned many awards for her teaching. She has been praised for bringing music to the children of New York City. Her music program began in just one classroom. Now it brings music to thousands of children.

The Music of Life (continued)

Comprehension Activity

Circle the letter of the best answer for each question.

1 What kind of writing is this selection?
- a. fiction
- b. nonfiction
- c. fantasy

2 From what you read, which word best describes Roberta Guaspari?
- a. quiet
- b. the outdoor-type
- c. firm

3 What happened after Ms. Guaspari was on TV to tell her story?
- a. Her music program ended.
- b. People donated money to keep the music program going.
- c. Other music teachers offered their time to keep the program going.

Learn About Words

Circle A, B, or C to choose the synonym of the underlined word.

1 Musicians donated their time and money.
- a. gave
- b. counted
- c. took

2 The music students have played for Presidents.
- a. voted
- b. met
- c. performed

3 They make something delightful with their music.
- a. ugly
- b. pleasing
- c. loud

| apologized | pouted | request | shelter | volunteers |

Gabby Learns a Lesson

Gabby was used to getting things her way all the time. If there was a new toy she wanted, her mother and father got it for her. After school every day, she got to do whatever she wanted. She never had to help around the house, and she never had to do any chores at all. You might say that Gabby was a spoiled, selfish child.

Since Gabby always got her way, you might also think that she was happy with her life. Instead, Gabby was unhappy and she pouted all the time. The more she got, the more she thought she should get. She expected her friends to do what she wanted all the time. She thought her friends should share with her, but she didn't share with them. One by one, her friends stopped spending time with her. Gabby couldn't understand why her friends didn't want to be around her anymore. She didn't see that the way she treated her friends drove them away.

One Saturday, Gabby was pouting because she had no friends to play with her. Her mom was getting ready to go help at a shelter for homeless people. She helped serve lunch almost every Saturday. Since Gabby had nothing else to do, she asked her mom if she could go too. Gabby's mom was stunned by Gabby's request. She told Gabby that she would be expected to help serve lunch,

and no one would be serving her. Gabby's mom was even more shocked when Gabby said, "Okay. Let's go."

When they got to the shelter, Gabby saw children waiting with their parents for a hot meal. Gabby worked very hard to help her mom and the other volunteers who were serving lunch to the families.

When Gabby took a break, she watched the families eating together. They talked and laughed while they ate. Although they didn't have a lot of things, they seemed happy. It made Gabby feel good to think that she helped bring smiles to their faces. It was then that Gabby realized that this good feeling was something new for her.

When Gabby got home, she thought for a long time about how she had been acting. She knew she had not been very nice to her friends. She apologized to her parents for pouting and for not helping them more. She wanted to make a change. From then on, Gabby helped her mom at the shelter every Saturday. She smiled instead of pouted and she was kind and shared her toys. She won back her old friends, and she made new friends too. Gabby had learned an important lesson.

Gabby Learns a Lesson (continued)

Comprehension Activity

Circle the letter of the best answer for each question.

1 Which word describes Gabby at the beginning of the story?
  a. kind
  b. spoiled *(circled)*
  c. forgetful

2 What happens after Gabby helps at the shelter?
  a. She changes the way she acts. *(circled)*
  b. She never goes to the shelter again.
  c. She goes home and plays with her toys.

3 What lesson does Gabby learn in this story?
  a. It's nice to get your own way.
  b. Help yourself, not others.
  c. Helping others makes you feel good. *(circled)*

Learn About Words

Read each sentence. Then circle the letter for the word in the sentence that contains a suffix.

1 At the end of the story, Gabby is a helpful child.
  a. helpful *(circled)*
  b. story
  c. end

2 Gabby's mom kindly helps out at the shelter.
  a. shelter
  b. out
  c. kindly *(circled)*

3 Someone who doesn't share might be a selfish person.
  a. selfish *(circled)*
  b. doesn't
  c. someone

---

camera	computer	cousin	museum	photography

A Family Story

Eddie was interested in photography. He loved to read books about it. He liked looking at old family photos. He often went to the photography shows at the museum. On Eddie's birthday, he got the gift he really wanted. He got a camera.

Eddie wanted his photos to be interesting and fun. He wanted his photos to tell a story. Eddie looked around him. He saw new leaves on the trees. He saw spring flowers on the bushes. It was all very pretty, but it was not what Eddie wanted to show in his photos.

Eddie's mom and dad were planting flowers in the garden. Eddie's sister, Amanda, was riding her bike around and around. This was neither fun nor interesting. This was everyday stuff.

Then Eddie heard Mom laugh. She had slipped in the garden. She was sitting in the dirt. Eddie snapped a picture! As Dad helped Mom stand up, Dad slipped too. Now they were both sitting in the dirt. They were both laughing. Eddie snapped another picture.

Suddenly Amanda rode up close to Eddie. She yelled, "Take a picture of me! Try to catch me!" Eddie pushed the button as Amanda zoomed away.

Eddie took more pictures that day. He took a photo of his aunt and uncle as they drove up in

their car. He took a photo of his cousins getting out of the car. He took a photo of his oldest cousin holding his new baby cousin. Eddie even took a picture of himself. He held his arms out as far as he could. He aimed the camera at his face. Snap!

That evening, Eddie linked the camera up to the computer. This way he could see the photos on the screen. Eddie smiled. Here were the things that had happened that day. Amanda's hair was flying out as she rode her bike. Mom and Dad were laughing like kids in the garden. His aunt and uncle were waving from the car window. His cousins were hopping around the car. Eddie was smiling straight into the camera.

Eddie's photos told a story about his family. He printed the photos on the printer. He made a book of blank pages. On each page he put a photo. Then he wrote about each photo. Eddie gave the book to his grandmother.

Eddie and his grandmother sat together to read Eddie's story about their family. Grandmother smiled. She said this was the best story she had ever read.

A Family Story (continued)

Comprehension Activity

Circle A, B, or C.

1 Which sentence best tells the main idea of this selection?
  a. It's fun to take pictures.
  b. Pictures can tell a story. *(circled)*
  c. Eddie is a nice son.

2 At the end of the story, what does Eddie understand about his photos?
  a. He understands that taking photos is not interesting.
  b. He understands that his photos are pretty.
  c. He understands that his photos could tell a story. *(circled)*

3 Which sentence tells you that Eddie's grandmother liked what Eddie did?
  a. Eddie gave the book to his grandmother.
  b. Eddie and his grandmother sat together.
  c. Grandmother said this was the best story she had ever read. *(circled)*

Learn About Words

Circle A, B, or C to choose the part of speech of the underlined word.

1 Mom does not like having her picture taken.
  a. verb
  b. noun *(circled)*
  c. adjective

2 Eddie took a picture of himself.
  a. verb *(circled)*
  b. noun
  c. adjective

3 He took a photo of his oldest cousin.
  a. verb
  b. noun
  c. adjective *(circled)*

---

dolphins	guides	healthier	muscles	seizure

Animal Helpers

You might have heard about dogs that work as guides for people who are blind. You might know about dogs that help people who are in wheelchairs. Do you know that there are other ways that dogs can help people? Do you know that there are other helpful animals, too? Would you be shocked to know that monkeys, horses, and dolphins can help people, too?

Some dogs have an important talent. They can sense when a person is going to have a seizure. No one knows what gives some dogs this unusual talent. Some people who have seizures have found that their dog knows that they are about to be ill. The dog barks or gives a warning to let the person know that they should sit or lie down. The dog then stays with the person until the seizure is over.

Some monkeys can be trained to help people, too. Because monkeys have hands like people do, they can do many things that dogs cannot do. They can pick up things, turn the pages of a book or turn on a light. They help people who cannot do these things for themselves. Monkeys, like other animals, often enjoy being with people. A person with a helpful monkey usually thinks of the monkey as a good friend.

Animals can also help people be healthier. A horse is one such animal. A horse can help people make their muscles stronger. When you walk, you use muscles in your legs and in your sides. These muscles are the same ones you use when riding a horse. When people ride horses, their side muscles get stronger. Stronger side muscles make walking easier. Children who have trouble walking can enjoy the freedom of movement while riding a horse. As they ride, they also make their muscles stronger.

The dolphin is another animal that can help people feel better. Dolphins are very smart animals. They can be trained to let people swim with them. Children and adults who swim with dolphins often feel better about themselves. Most people who swim with dolphins say that it makes them feel happy. Some people are able to do more than they thought they could when they swim with dolphins.

If you have a pet, you know how happy your pet can make you. Now you know that animals not only help make us happy. They can also help us do more and be healthier.

Animal Helpers (continued)

Comprehension Activity

Circle the letter of the best answer for each question.

1 Which sentence best tells the main idea of this selection?
  a. Many animals can help people.
  b. Most people love their pets.
  c. Some people have helpful monkeys.

2 How does riding a horse help people?
  a. Riding helps people like horses.
  b. Riding makes muscles stronger.
  c. Horses make good pets.

3 Based on the information in the selection, which statement is true?
  a. Dolphins make people feel sad.
  b. Monkeys are smart animals.
  c. Horses are smarter than dogs.

Learn About Words

Circle A, B, or C.

1 Which set of words is in alphabetical order?
  a. people, friend, sit
  b. sit, friend, people
  c. friend, people, sit

2 Which word goes between *dog* and *walk* so that the three words are in alphabetical order?

  dog, _____, walk
  a. animal
  b. legs
  c. you

3 Which set of words is NOT in alphabetical order?
  a. work, swim, bark
  b. book, healthy, smart
  c. dolphin, happy, pet

Animal Helpers **75**

---

control	glider	lever	scientists	Orville and Wilbur Wright

A History of Flight

Have you ever been flying in an airplane? Today air travel is a fast way to get people and things to faraway places. Air travel even took men to the moon. But people did not always fly. In fact, airplanes have been around for just over 100 years.

People first took to the skies in hot-air balloons. The heated air in the big balloon made the balloon go up in the air. People rode in a basket that hung under the balloon. It was hard to control how the hot-air balloon moved. Riders had to travel where the wind took them.

The next air travel invention was the glider. Gliders had to take off from a high place. Again, the gliders could only go where the wind and air took them. The first gliders could not hold a lot of weight. They could not go far. They could not fly on a calm day. Many people worked to make the glider better.

At the end of the 1800s, two brothers named Orville and Wilbur Wright tried to build an airplane. It was powered by an engine, not powered by the wind. The first flight of their airplane was December 17, 1903. In this first airplane flight, the pilot rode on the lower wing. He controlled the airplane with his hips and a hand lever.

Within ten years, pilots were flying airplanes in races. They would fly from one city to another. Everyone wanted airplanes that could fly higher, farther, and faster. Airplane companies around the world began to build airplanes.

Airplanes were first used in battle during World War I. This was around 1914. Today, airplanes fly higher, farther, and faster than those first airplanes. Even the spacecraft of today are based on the ideas of the first airplanes. As you know, spacecraft fly the highest, farthest, and fastest of all.

People are still making airplanes better. Scientists are working on airplanes that fix themselves if something breaks during a flight. Some airplanes are getting better computers. This can help pilots know what is happening around the airplane. They will know what is going on no matter how dark it is or how bad the weather is. Scientists are also trying to make better personal airplanes. This is a plane for just one person. People can fly this airplane without much training. One day you might fly to work or to school. Can you imagine a sky full of airplanes instead of a road full of cars?

76 *A History of Flight*

A History of Flight (continued)

Comprehension Activity

Circle the letter of the best answer for each question.

1 Which sentence BEST tells the main idea of this selection?
  a. Airplanes have changed a lot.
  b. Airplanes are fun to ride in.
  c. Airplanes were invented over 100 years ago.

2 How has the invention of the airplane changed people's lives?
  a. Everyone flies in personal airplanes.
  b. People can travel farther and faster.
  c. Everyone lives near an airport.

3 How might air travel be different one day?
  a. It might be easy for everyone to fly a plane.
  b. The roads will be filled with airplanes.
  c. People will ride in a basket under a balloon.

Learn About Words

Circle A, B, or C to choose the synonym of the underlined adjective.

1 Today air travel is a <u>fast</u> way to travel.
  a. friendly
  b. slow
  c. quick

2 Gliders could not fly on a <u>calm</u> day.
  a. clean
  b. windless
  c. rough

3 Scientists are also trying to make <u>better</u> personal airplanes.
  a. bad
  b. bitter
  c. greater

A History of Flight **77**

Gianni	liberty	Lucia	Napoli, Italy	Paulo

Going to America in 1898

Paulo and Anna lived in a tiny town in the south of Italy. Their children were Gianni and Lucia. Gianni was ten years old and Lucia was eight years old. They had never lived anywhere else. Paulo was a baker. He did not make much money because the people in town were so poor.

Anna said to Paulo that they might all have a better life in America. They packed two large trunks with everything they owned. Gianni thought it would be a great adventure. Lucia was afraid of being around so many people she did not know.

They took a train to the sea. The children had never been on a train before. At the city of Napoli they met their steamship. Lucia said the ship looked as long as a whole row of houses in their town.

Paulo and his family stayed on a lower deck of the ship. Many of the other people spoke Italian but some did not. Paulo and Gianni slept on bunk beds in a room with the other men. Anna and Lucia stayed with the women. They all ate at long tables. Sometimes people played music and danced. Gianni played games with other boys.

One morning after many long days at sea, Paulo and his family stood on the deck of the ship. The sea was very calm. The sun was rising behind them, and the sky was a clear blue. Birds flew overhead, rising and falling with the wind. All of a sudden they saw Lady Liberty. They had arrived in America.

Two hours later the ship stopped at a large dock. Paulo's family climbed down a ramp behind many other people. A sign read "Ellis Island." A huge crowd of people waited to show papers before passing through an iron gate. To Paulo that crowd seemed as large as the ocean they had just crossed. Paulo and his family waited for their turn.

Finally Paulo and his family rode a much smaller boat from the island. They climbed a set of stone stairs. At the top they discovered a street with lots of very tall buildings. The street was alive with crowds, and there was a lot of noise as people passed Paulo and his family.

"Well, my dears," said Paulo. "We are in our new home. This is America!"

Comprehension Activity

Circle the letter of the best answer for each question.

1 Why did Paulo and Anna move to America?
  a. They had once lived in America.
  b. Gianni and Lucia did not like Italy.
  c. They hoped for a better life.

2 How did Gianni feel about going to America?
  a. He thought it would be an adventure.
  b. He just didn't want to go.
  c. He was afraid.

3 What did Lucia say about the steamship?
  a. It did not look safe.
  b. It looked like the ships docked in their town.
  c. It looked as long as a whole row of houses in their town.

78 *Going to America in 1898*

Going to America in 1898 (continued)

4. How did Paulo and his family get to the steamship?
   a. They walked to the steamship.
   (b.) They took a train to the steamship.
   c. They took a horse and buggy to the steamship.

5. How was the trip to the steamship different for the children?
   (a.) They had never been on a train before.
   b. The children did not like it.
   c. They slept in different rooms.

6. How did Paulo's family know they had reached America?
   a. They saw an island.
   b. The captain told them.
   (c.) They saw Lady Liberty.

7. What did the family do right after they got off the ship?
   a. They got into a smaller boat.
   (b.) They went to Ellis Island.
   c. They took a train ride.

8. To what did Paulo compare the crowd at Ellis Island?
   a. The crowd looked like animals on a farm.
   (b.) The crowd looked like the ocean they had just crossed.
   c. The crowd looked like the people from their town in Italy.

9. Where was Paulo's family's new home?
   (a.) America
   b. Napoli
   c. Ellis Island

Going to America in 1898 (continued)

Learn About Words

Look at each number in parentheses. Find the paragraph in the story with the same number. Then find the word that fits the given meaning. Write your answers on the lines.

1. a fun thing to do (2) ___adventure___

2. freedom to think and act without fear (5) ___liberty___

3. a sloping walkway (6) ___ramp___

4. a piece of land with water all around it (6) ___island___

5. found (7) ___discovered___

Scope and Sequence
Decoding B2

Scope and Sequence

Lesson Objectives

Lesson Objectives	Lesson 1	Lesson 2	Lesson 3	Lesson 4	Lesson 5	Lesson 6	Lesson 7	Lesson 8	Lesson 9
Sound Combinations	X	X	X					X	
Letter Combinations/Letter Sounds				X	X	X	X	X	X
Final E Rule	X	X	X	X	X				
Suffixes	X		X	X		X			
Contractions					X				X
Visual Discrimination									
Multisyllabic Words									
Word Recognition	X	X	X	X	X	X	X	X	X
High-Frequency Words	X	X	X	X	X	X	X	X	X
Assessment									
Ongoing: Individual Tests	X	X	X	X	X	X	X	X	X
Group Reading									
Decoding and Word Analysis									
Read Decodable Text	X	X	X	X	X	X	X	X	X
Comprehension									
Access Prior Knowledge	X	X	X	X	X	X	X	X	X
Draw Inferences	X	X	X	X	X	X	X	X	X
Note Details	X	X	X	X	X	X	X	X	X
Predict	X	X	X	X	X	X	X	X	X
Assessment									
Ongoing: Comprehension Check	X	X	X	X	X	X	X	X	X
Ongoing: Decoding Accuracy	X	X	X	X	X	X	X	X	X
Formal									
Fluency Assessments									
Fluency									
Reread Decodable Text	X	X	X	X	X	X	X	X	X
Assessment									
Ongoing: Teacher-Monitored Accuracy	X	X	X	X	X	X	X	X	X
Ongoing: Peer-Monitored Accuracy	X	X	X	X	X	X	X	X	X
Ongoing: Teacher-Monitored Fluency		X	X	X	X	X	X	X	X
Ongoing: Peer-Monitored Fluency		X	X	X	X	X	X	X	X
Workbook Exercises									
Decoding and Word Analysis									
Spelling: Sound/Letter Relationships	X	X	X		X	X	X	X	X
Spelling: Suffixes and Final E	X	X	X	X	X	X	X	X	X
Spelling: Roots and Suffixes									
Spelling: Multisyllabic Words		X	X		X		X		
Spelling: Compound Words									
Visual Discrimination	X								
Comprehension									
Main Idea									
Sequencing				X					X
Following Written Directions	X	X	X		X	X	X	X	
Identify Characters					X				
Modified Cloze									
Picture Comprehension									
Note Details	X	X	X	X	X	X	X	X	X
Note Details: Who, What, When, Where					X	X	X	X	
Study Skills									
Writing Mechanics	X	X			X	X	X		
Assessment									
Ongoing: Workcheck	X	X	X	X	X	X	X	X	X

Scope and Sequence (cont'd)

Lesson 10	Lesson 11	Lesson 12	Lesson 13	Lesson 14	Lesson 15	Lesson 16	Lesson 17	Lesson 18	Lesson 19	Lesson 20
X	X		X	X	X	X	X			X
X	X	X	X	X	X	X	X	X	X	X
								X		
X									X	
						X			X	
X	X	X	X	X	X	X	X	X	X	X
X	X	X	X	X	X	X	X	X	X	X
X	X	X	X	X	X	X	X	X	X	X
X				X	X	X				X
X	X	X	X	X	X	X	X	X	X	X
X	X	X	X	X	X	X	X	X	X	X
X	X	X	X	X	X	X	X	X	X	X
X	X	X	X	X	X	X	X	X	X	X
X	X	X	X	X	X	X	X	X	X	X
X										X
X	X	X	X	X	X	X	X	X	X	X
X	X	X	X	X	X	X	X	X	X	X
X	X	X	X	X	X	X	X	X	X	X
X	X	X	X	X	X	X	X	X	X	X
X	X	X	X	X	X	X	X	X	X	X
X	X	X	X			X				
	X	X		X	X		X	X	X	X
X						X	X			
			X							
X	X		X			X				
		X							X	
	X		X	X	X		X			X
X			X					X		
	X	X		X	X	X	X	X	X	X
X				X			X			
	X		X	X	X	X	X			X
X	X	X	X	X		X	X	X	X	X

Scope and Sequence

Lesson Objectives	Lesson 21	Lesson 22	Lesson 23	Lesson 24	Lesson 25	Lesson 26	Lesson 27	Lesson 28	Lesson 29
Sound Combinations	X	X	X						
Letter Combinations/Letter Sounds	X	X	X	X	X	X	X	X	X
Final E Rule									
Suffixes									
Contractions									
Visual Discrimination						X	X	X	X
Multisyllabic Words	X			X					
Word Recognition		X	X	X	X	X	X	X	X
High-Frequency Words	X		X	X			X	X	
Assessment									
Ongoing: Individual Tests	X	X	X	X	X	X	X	X	X
Group Reading									
Decoding and Word Analysis									
Read Decodable Text	X	X	X	X	X	X	X	X	X
Comprehension									
Access Prior Knowledge	X	X	X						
Draw Inferences	X	X	X	X	X	X	X	X	X
Note Details	X	X	X	X	X	X	X	X	X
Predict	X	X	X	X	X	X	X	X	X
Assessment									
Ongoing: Comprehension Check	X	X	X	X	X	X	X	X	X
Ongoing: Decoding Accuracy	X	X	X	X	X	X	X	X	X
Formal									
Fluency Assessments									
Fluency									
Reread Decodable Text	X	X	X	X	X	X	X	X	X
Assessment									
Ongoing: Teacher-Monitored Accuracy	X	X	X	X	X	X	X	X	X
Ongoing: Peer-Monitored Accuracy	X	X	X	X	X	X	X	X	X
Ongoing: Teacher-Monitored Fluency	X	X	X	X	X	X	X	X	X
Ongoing: Peer-Monitored Fluency	X	X	X	X	X	X	X	X	X
Workbook Exercises									
Decoding and Word Analysis									
Spelling: Sound/Letter Relationships		X	X						
Spelling: Suffixes and Final E		X			X		X		X
Spelling: Roots and Suffixes			X			X	X		X
Spelling: Multisyllabic Words	X					X		X	
Spelling: Compound Words						X		X	
Visual Discrimination		X	X						
Comprehension									
Main Idea									X
Sequencing							X		
Following Written Directions								X	
Identify Characters									X
Modified Cloze									
Picture Comprehension									
Note Details						X	X	X	
Note Details: Who, What, When, Where						X			X
Study Skills									
Writing Mechanics		X		X	X				X
Assessment									
Ongoing: Workcheck	X	X	X	X	X	X	X	X	X

Scope and Sequence (cont'd)

Lesson 30	Lesson 31	Lesson 32	Lesson 33	Lesson 34	Lesson 35	Lesson 36	Lesson 37	Lesson 38	Lesson 39	Lesson 40
X	X						X	X		X
	X	X	X	X		X	X	X	X	
		X	X	X					X	
	X	X	X	X		X	X		X	X
							X			
X	X	X	X	X	X	X	X	X	X	X
				X	X		X	X	X	X
X	X	X	X	X	X	X	X	X	X	X
X	X	X	X	X	X	X	X	X	X	X
X	X	X		X						
X	X	X	X	X	X	X	X	X	X	X
X	X	X	X	X	X	X	X	X	X	X
X	X	X	X	X	X	X	X	X	X	X
X	X	X	X	X	X	X	X	X	X	X
X	X	X	X	X	X	X	X	X	X	X
X										X
X	X	X	X	X	X	X	X	X	X	X
X	X	X	X	X	X	X	X	X	X	X
X	X	X	X	X	X	X	X	X	X	X
X	X	X	X	X	X	X	X	X	X	X
X	X	X	X	X	X	X	X	X	X	X
X					X	X			X	
		X			X					
		X	X			X				
	X			X				X	X	
X					X	X			X	
							X			X
		X					X			
X			X						X	X
			X	X	X			X	X	
	X									X
X	X	X	X	X	X	X	X	X		X
								X		
	X						X	X	X	X
X	X	X	X	X	X	X	X	X	X	X

Scope and Sequence

Lesson Objectives

Lesson Objectives	Lesson 41	Lesson 42	Lesson 43	Lesson 44	Lesson 45	Lesson 46	Lesson 47	Lesson 48	Lesson 49
Sound Combinations							X	X	X
Letter Combinations/Letter Sounds	X	X	X		X	X	X	X	X
Final E Rule									
Suffixes									
Contractions					X				
Visual Discrimination		X	X		X		X		X
Multisyllabic Words			X			X		X	
Word Recognition	X	X	X	X	X	X	X	X	X
High-Frequency Words	X	X	X	X		X	X	X	X
Assessment									
Ongoing: Individual Tests	X	X	X	X	X	X	X	X	X
Group Reading									
Decoding and Word Analysis									
Read Decodable Text	X	X	X	X	X	X	X	X	X
Comprehension									
Access Prior Knowledge	X		X	X					X
Draw Inferences	X	X	X	X	X	X	X	X	X
Note Details	X	X	X	X	X	X	X	X	X
Predict	X	X	X	X	X	X	X	X	X
Assessment									
Ongoing: Comprehension Check	X	X	X	X	X	X	X	X	X
Ongoing: Decoding Accuracy	X	X	X	X	X	X	X	X	X
Formal									
Fluency Assessments									
Fluency									
Reread Decodable Text	X	X	X	X	X	X	X	X	X
Assessment									
Ongoing: Teacher-Monitored Accuracy	X	X	X	X	X	X	X	X	X
Ongoing: Peer-Monitored Accuracy	X	X	X	X	X	X	X	X	X
Ongoing: Teacher-Monitored Fluency	X	X	X	X	X	X	X	X	X
Ongoing: Peer-Monitored Fluency	X	X	X	X	X	X	X	X	X
Workbook Exercises									
Decoding and Word Analysis									
Spelling: Sound/Letter Relationships					X		X		
Spelling: Suffixes and Final E					X	X		X	
Spelling: Roots and Suffixes	X	X	X	X	X	X		X	
Spelling: Multisyllabic Words									
Spelling: Compound Words						X			X
Visual Discrimination				X			X		
Comprehension									
Main Idea							X		
Sequencing		X						X	
Following Written Directions	X			X	X				
Identify Characters			X				X		
Modified Cloze		X					X		
Picture Comprehension					X		X		X
Note Details	X	X	X		X		X	X	X
Note Details: Who, What, When, Where				X					
Study Skills									
Writing Mechanics	X			X	X	X			
Assessment									
Ongoing: Workcheck	X	X	X	X	X	X	X	X	X

100   *Scope and Sequence*   *Corrective Reading*

Scope and Sequence (cont'd)

Lesson 50	Lesson 51	Lesson 52	Lesson 53	Lesson 54	Lesson 55	Lesson 56	Lesson 57	Lesson 58	Lesson 59	Lesson 60
X		X	X	X	X					
X	X	X	X			X	X	X		X
X	X				X					
	X	X				X		X	X	X
X	X	X	X	X	X	X	X	X	X	X
	X	X	X	X	X	X	X	X	X	
X	X	X	X	X	X	X	X	X	X	X
X	X	X	X	X	X	X	X	X	X	X
X				X						
X	X	X	X	X	X	X	X	X	X	X
X	X	X	X	X	X	X	X	X	X	X
X	X	X	X	X	X	X	X	X	X	X
X	X	X	X	X	X	X	X	X	X	X
X	X	X	X	X	X	X	X	X	X	X
X										
X	X	X	X	X	X	X	X	X	X	X
X	X	X	X	X	X	X	X	X	X	X
X	X	X	X	X	X	X	X	X	X	X
X	X	X	X	X	X	X	X	X	X	X
X	X	X	X	X	X	X	X	X	X	X
				X				X	X	
		X			X			X		X
X		X			X		X	X		X
			X						X	X
				X				X	X	
	X									
				X					X	
		X			X	X	X		X	X
		X			X	X				X
	X		X	X			X		X	
X		X			X		X	X	X	
X		X	X		X	X				
	X	X			X	X				X
X	X	X	X	X	X	X	X	X	X	X

Scope and Sequence

Lesson Objectives	Lesson 61	Lesson 62	Lesson 63	Lesson 64	Lesson 65
Sound Combinations					
Letter Combinations/Letter Sounds		X	X	X	X
Final E Rule					
Suffixes					
Contractions					
Visual Discrimination			X		X
Multisyllabic Words	X	X		X	
Word Recognition	X	X	X	X	X
High-Frequency Words	X	X	X	X	
Assessment					
Ongoing: Individual Tests	X	X	X	X	X
Group Reading					
Decoding and Word Analysis					
Read Decodable Text	X	X	X	X	X
Comprehension					
Access Prior Knowledge					
Draw Inferences	X	X	X	X	X
Note Details	X	X	X	X	X
Predict	X	X	X	X	X
Assessment					
Ongoing: Comprehension Check	X	X	X	X	X
Ongoing: Decoding Accuracy	X	X	X	X	X
Formal					X
Fluency Assessments					
Fluency					
Reread Decodable Text	X	X	X	X	X
Assessment					
Ongoing: Teacher-Monitored Accuracy	X	X	X	X	X
Ongoing: Peer-Monitored Accuracy	X	X	X	X	X
Ongoing: Teacher-Monitored Fluency	X	X	X	X	X
Ongoing: Peer-Monitored Fluency	X	X	X	X	X
Workbook Exercises					
Decoding and Word Analysis					
Spelling: Sound/Letter Relationships			X		X
Spelling: Suffixes and Final E	X				
Spelling: Roots and Suffixes	X			X	
Spelling: Multisyllabic Words					
Spelling: Compound Words		X		X	
Visual Discrimination			X		X
Comprehension					
Main Idea					
Sequencing			X	X	
Following Written Directions	X				
Identify Characters					
Modified Cloze					
Picture Comprehension		X	X		
Note Details	X	X	X	X	X
Note Details: Who, What, When, Where	X	X			X
Study Skills					
Writing Mechanics	X				
Assessment					
Ongoing: Workcheck	X	X	X	X	X

Objectives

Objectives	The Homework Handshake	How Is the Weather?	Follow Your Nose, Dog!	Watch That Melon
Vocabulary/Language				
Comprehend Word Usage				
Deduct Meaning from Context Clues				
Define Words				
Identify Contractions				
Identify Parts of Speech				
Identify Synonyms or Antonyms				
Identify Word Parts—Prefixes/Suffixes/Root Words				
Reading Comprehension Strategy/ Skills				
Cause and Effect				
Classify				
Compare and Contrast				
Follow Directions	x	x	x	x
Identify Alphabetical Order				
Identify Fact/Fiction				
Identify Main Idea				
Identify or Describe Character Qualities				
Identify Problem/Solution/Effect				x
Identify True/False				
Illustrate Story Events		x		
Make Connections				
Make Deductions	x	x	x	x
Make Inferences and Draw Conclusions			x	
Make Predictions				
Present Evidence	x	x	x	x
Recall Story Details	x	x	x	x
Sequence Events	x			
Summarize			x	x

Rodney, The Inventor Who Never Gave Up	The Red Kangaroo	Fit Body, Fit Mind	Lady Baseball	A New Start	Making a Difference	Horses of America
				x	X	x
x	x					
x	x	x	x	x	X	x
x						
x	x	x				
x	x	x		x	X	x
x	x	x	x			
x	x	x	x	x	X	x
				x		

Scope and Sequence

Objectives

Objectives	The Case of the Missing Bear	Antarctica	Sledding with Grandpa	Carl's Summer on the Farm
Vocabulary/Language				
Comprehend Word Usage			x	
Deduct Meaning from Context Clues				
Define Words				
Identify Contractions				
Identify Parts of Speech	x			
Identify Synonyms or Antonyms		x		X
Identify Word Parts—Prefixes/Suffixes/Root Words				
Reading Comprehension Strategy/ Skills				
Cause and Effect				
Classify				
Compare and Contrast				
Follow Directions	x	x	x	X
Identify Alphabetical Order				
Identify Fact/Fiction				
Identify Main Idea		x		
Identify or Describe Character Qualities				
Identify Problem/Solution/Effect				
Identify True/False				
Illustrate Story Events				
Make Connections				
Make Deductions	x	x	x	X
Make Inferences and Draw Conclusions				
Make Predictions				
Present Evidence				
Recall Story Details	x	x	x	X
Sequence Events				
Summarize				

Scope and Sequence (cont'd)

Thomas Edison	The Planets in Our Solar System	Beachcombing	At Work in the Forest	The Lion and the Mouse	The Music of Life	Gabby Learns a Lesson
X						
	X	X				
X						
				X		
					X	
X			X			X
X			X			
		X				
				X		
X	X	X	X	X	X	X
					X	
X	X					
				X		X
				X		
X	X	X	X		X	X
	X	X		X		
X						
X	X	X	X		X	X
					X	X
X				X		X

Scope and Sequence

Objectives

Objectives	A Family Story	Animal Helpers	A History of Flight	Going to America
Vocabulary/Language				
Comprehend Word Usage				
Deduct Meaning from Context Clues				x
Define Words				
Identify Contractions				
Identify Parts of Speech	x			
Identify Synonyms or Antonyms			x	
Identify Word Parts—Prefixes/Suffixes/Root Words				
Reading Comprehension Strategy/ Skills				
Cause and Effect				
Classify				
Compare and Contrast				
Follow Directions	x	x	x	x
Identify Alphabetical Order		x		
Identify Fact/Fiction				
Identify Main Idea	x	x	x	
Identify or Describe Character Qualities				
Identify Problem/Solution/Effect				
Identify True/False		x		
Illustrate Story Events				
Make Connections				
Make Deductions	x	x	x	x
Make Inferences and Draw Conclusions				
Make Predictions			x	
Present Evidence	x			
Recall Story Details	x	x	x	x
Sequence Events				
Summarize				

Scope and Sequence

Lesson Objectives

Lesson Objectives	Lesson 1	Lesson 2	Lesson 3	Lesson 4
Vocabulary/Language				
Comprehend Word Usage	X	X	X	X
Define Vocabulary Words	X	X	X	X
Identify Parts of Speech	X	X	X	X
Reading Comprehension Strategy/Skills				
Activate Prior Knowledge				X
Build Background	X	X	X	X
Compare and Contrast				
Demonstrate Understanding Through Physical Response				X
Develop Listening Skills	X	X	X	X
Explore Content Through a Variety of Media		X		
Identify Cause and Effect				
Identify Fact and Opinion				X
Identify Problem/Solution/Effect	X			
Identify True or False				X
Make Connections				
Make Inferences and Draw Conclusions	X	X		X
Make Judgments	X			X
Make Predictions	X			
Note Story Details	X	X	X	X
Present Evidence: Facts		X	X	X
Sequence Events			X	
Take Notes/Illustrate Story Events	X	X	X	X
Use Deductive Reasoning	X			X
Use Knowledge to Complete Graphic Organizers	X	X	X	X
Visualize Story Events		X		
Literary Analysis				
Identify and Describe Characters	X	X		
Identify Elements of a Plot—Problem, Action, Climax, Resolution	X			
Identify Figurative Language				
Identify Genre—Fact/Fiction			X	
Identify Genre—Poetry	X			
Identify Genre—Parody				
Identify Genre—Personal Narrative				
Identify Genre—Tall Tales				
Identify Setting—Time, Place, Culture	X			

Lesson 5	Lesson 6	Lesson 7	Lesson 8	Lesson 9	Lesson 10	Lesson 11	Lesson 12
X	X	X	X	X	X	X	X
X	X	X	X	X	X	X	X
X	X	X	X	X	X	X	X
	X						X
X	X	X	X	X	X	X	X
				X	X		
X	X	X	X	X	X	X	X
	X				X		
X							
	X		X				
X							
		X		X	X		X
	X	X					X
		X		X			
X	X	X	X	X	X	X	X
	X			X		X	
			X			X	
X	X	X	X	X	X	X	X
X				X			X
X	X	X	X	X	X	X	X
					X		
		X				X	X
		X					
	X	X					
		X					
							X
	X						
		X					
						X	

Type of Text—Narrative	Building Background	Chapter 1	Chapter 2	Chapter 3	Chapter 4	Chapter 5	Chapter 6	Thinking & Writing
				Thousand-Mile Words				
VOCABULARY INSTRUCTION								
Explicit Instruction		X	X	X	X	X	X	X
Word Learning Strategies (morphemic/contextual analysis)		X	X	X	X	X	X	
COMPREHENSION STRATEGIES/SKILLS (before-, during-, after-reading)								
Graphic Organizers								X
Comprehension Monitoring		X	X	X	X	X	X	
Background Knowledge	X							
Sequencing		X			X			
Opinion / Evaluation	X			X				X
Recall Facts and Details		X	X	X	X	X	X	X
Story Grammar (Character, Plot, Setting)		X						
Cause and Effect						X		X
Inferences						X		
Drawing Conclusions			X	X	X	X	X	
FLUENCY								
Fluency Practice		X	X	X	X	X	X	
Fluency Assessment		X					X	

Scope and Sequence (cont'd)

Ravenscourt Readers Decoding B2

They Landed One Night

Type of Text—Narrative	Building Background	Chapter 1	Chapter 2	Chapter 3	Chapter 4	Chapter 5	Chapter 6	Thinking & Writing
VOCABULARY INSTRUCTION								
Explicit Instruction		X	X	X	X	X	X	
Word Learning Strategies (morphemic/contextual analysis)		X	X	X	X	X	X	
COMPREHENSION STRATEGIES/SKILLS (before-, during-, after-reading)								
Graphic Organizers								X
Comprehension Monitoring		X	X	X	X	X	X	
Background Knowledge	X							X
Predictions					X			
Sequencing			X			X		
Opinion / Evaluation	X	X				X		X
Recall Facts and Details		X	X	X	X	X	X	X
Cause and Effect				X			X	
Drawing Conclusions		X	X		X			
FLUENCY								
Fluency Practice		X	X	X	X	X	X	
Fluency Assessment		X		X				

Scope and Sequence

Ravenscourt Readers Decoding B2

Type of Text—Narrative	Building Background	Bidding on the Past						Thinking & Writing
		Chapter 1	Chapter 2	Chapter 3	Chapter 4	Chapter 5	Chapter 6	
VOCABULARY INSTRUCTION								
Explicit Instruction		X	X	X	X	X	X	X
Word Learning Strategies (morphemic/contextual analysis)	X	X	X	X	X	X	X	
Reference: (online dictionary/thesaurus/atlas)	X							
COMPREHENSION STRATEGIES/SKILLS								
Graphic Organizers								X
Comprehension Monitoring		X	X	X	X	X	X	
Background Knowledge	X							
Compare/Contrast								X
Sequencing					X		X	
Opinion / Evaluation						X		X
Recall Facts and Details		X	X	X	X	X	X	X
Story Grammar (Character, Plot, Setting)		X						
Summarizing				X				
Cause and Effect				X				
Main Idea								X
Drawing Conclusions		X	X	X	X	X	X	
FLUENCY								
Fluency Practice		X	X	X	X	X	X	
Fluency Assessment			X		X			

Scope and Sequence (cont'd)

Ravenscourt Readers Decoding B2

Blues King: The Story of B.B.King

Type of Text –Expository	Building Background	Chapter 1	Chapter 2	Chapter 3	Chapter 4	Chapter 5	Chapter 6	Thinking & Writing
VOCABULARY INSTRUCTION								
Explicit Instruction		X	X	X	X	X	X	X
Word Learning Strategies (morphemic/contextual analysis)		X	X	X	X	X	X	X
COMPREHENSION STRATEGIES/SKILLS (before-, during-, and after-reading)								
Graphic Organizers								X
Comprehension Monitoring		X	X	X	X	X	X	
Background Knowledge	X							
Sequencing			X		X			
Opinion / Evaluation	X							X
Recall Facts and Details		X	X	X	X	X	X	X
Summarizing					X			
Cause and Effect						X	X	
Inferences					X			X
Drawing Conclusions		X	X					X
FLUENCY								
Fluency Practice		X	X	X	X	X	X	
Fluency Assessment				X			X	

Scope and Sequence

Ravenscourt Readers Decoding B2

Type of Text – Expository	Building Background	Chapter 1	Chapter 2	Chapter 3	Chapter 4	Chapter 5	Chapter 6	Thinking & Writing
VOCABULARY INSTRUCTION								
Explicit Instruction		X	X	X	X	X	X	
Word Learning Strategies (morphemic/contextual analysis)		X	X	X	X	X	X	
COMPREHENSION STRATEGIES/SKILLS (before-, during-, and after-reading)								
Graphic Organizers								X
Comprehension Monitoring		X	X	X	X	X	X	
Background Knowledge	X							
Compare/Contrast			X			X		X
Sequencing			X	X		X		
Opinion / Evaluation	X				X			X
Recall Facts and Details		X	X	X	X	X	X	X
Cause and Effect		X			X			
Inferences				X				
Drawing Conclusions							X	
FLUENCY								
Fluency Practice		X	X	X	X	X	X	
Fluency Assessment		X			X			

Scope and Sequence (cont'd)

Ravenscourt Readers Decoding B2

Art for All!

Type of Text –Expository	Building Background	Chapter 1	Chapter 2	Chapter 3	Chapter 4	Chapter 5	Chapter 6	Thinking & Writing
VOCABULARY INSTRUCTION								
Explicit Instruction		X	X	X	X	X	X	
Word Learning Strategies (morphemic/contextual analysis)		X	X	X	X	X	X	
COMPREHENSION STRATEGIES/SKILLS (before-, during-, and after-reading)								
Graphic Organizers								X
Comprehension Monitoring		X	X	X	X	X	X	
Background Knowledge	X							
Compare/Contrast	X			X				X
Sequencing								X
Opinion / Evaluation	X	X						X
Recall Facts and Details		X	X	X	X	X	X	X
Cause and Effect		X	X				X	X
Inferences			X					X
Drawing Conclusions		X					X	X
FLUENCY								
Fluency Practice		X	X	X	X	X	X	
Fluency Assessment			X		X			

Scope and Sequence

Ravenscourt Readers Decoding B2

Type of Text —Narrative	Building Background	Chapter 1	Chapter 2	Chapter 3	Chapter 4	Chapter 5	Chapter 6	Thinking & Writing
The Last Leaf and The Gift								
VOCABULARY INSTRUCTION								
Explicit Instruction		X	X	X	X	X	X	
Word Learning Strategies (morphemic/contextual analysis)		X	X	X	X	X	X	
COMPREHENSION STRATEGIES/SKILLS (before-, during-, and after-reading)								
Graphic Organizers								X
Comprehension Monitoring		X	X	X	X	X	X	
Background Knowledge	X							
Compare/Contrast	X					X		X
Sequencing			X	X		X		
Recall Facts and Details		X	X	X	X		X	X
Story Grammar (Character, Plot, Setting)			X					X
Summarizing								X
Cause and Effect		X			X	X	X	X
Inferences			X			X	X	
Drawing Conclusions			X	X	X	X		
FLUENCY								
Fluency Practice		X	X	X	X	X	X	
Fluency Assessment			X			X		

Scope and Sequence (cont'd)

Ravenscourt Readers Decoding B2

Type of Text --Narrative	Building Background	Oliver Twist						Thinking & Writing
		Chapter 1	Chapter 2	Chapter 3	Chapter 4	Chapter 5	Chapter 6	
VOCABULARY INSTRUCTION								
Explicit Instruction		X	X	X	X	X	X	
Word Learning Strategies (morphemic/contextual analysis)		X	X	X	X	X	X	
Reference: (online dictionary/thesaurus/atlas)	X							
COMPREHENSION STRATEGIES/SKILLS (before-, during-, and after-reading)								
Graphic Organizers	X							X
Comprehension Monitoring		X	X	X	X	X	X	
Background Knowledge	X							X
Predictions	X					X		X
Sequencing			X	X	X		X	
Opinion / Evaluation	X			X	X		X	X
Recall Facts and Details		X	X	X	X		X	X
Story Grammar (Character, Plot, Setting)					X			X
Cause and Effect		X	X	X	X	X		
Drawing Conclusions			X	X				X
FLUENCY								
Fluency Practice		X	X	X	X	X	X	
Fluency Assessment			X			X